Ramen Recipes

A Ramen Cookbook with Delicious Ramen Recipes

By
BookSumo Press
All rights reserved

Published by
http://www.booksumo.com

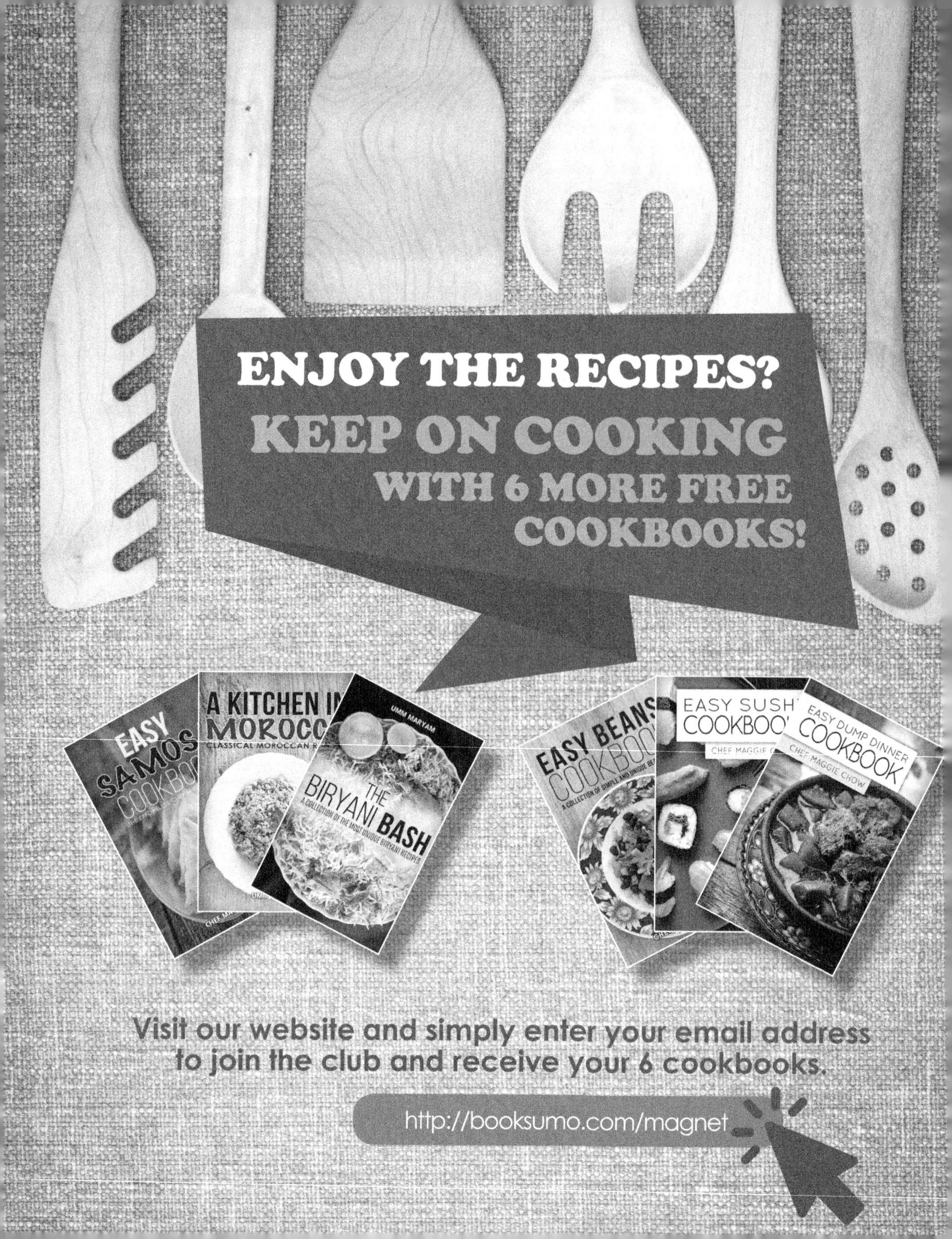

ENJOY THE RECIPES?
KEEP ON COOKING WITH 6 MORE FREE COOKBOOKS!

Visit our website and simply enter your email address to join the club and receive your 6 cookbooks.

http://booksumo.com/magnet

LEGAL NOTES

All Rights Reserved. No Part Of This Book May Be Reproduced Or Transmitted In Any Form Or By Any Means. Photocopying, Posting Online, And / Or Digital Copying Is Strictly Prohibited Unless Written Permission Is Granted By The Book's Publishing Company. Limited Use Of The Book's Text Is Permitted For Use In Reviews Written For The Public.

Table of Contents

4-Ingredient Ramen 9

Mung Bang Noodles Skillet 10

French Ramen Pan 11

Sweet Ramen Skillet 12

How to Make Miso Ramen 13

Marinated Eggs for Ramen 14

Apple Ramen Salad 15

Ramen Omelet 16

Ramen Seoul 17

Ramen Toscano 18

Sambal Ramen Salad 19

Chili Ramen Casserole 20

Broccoli and Oyster Ramen 21

Baby Ramen Soup 22

Shoyu Ramen 23

Ramen Green Bean Stir Fry 24

Mandarin Ramen Salad 25

Chili Coconut Ramen 26

Teriyaki Ramen Bowls 27

Ramen Steak Skillet 28

Parmesan Tuna Ramen 29

Ramen Sesame Soup 30

Sweet and Spicy Ramen Stir Fry 31

Lemongrass Ramen with Duck and Ginger 32

Creole Ramen 33

Fermented Sichuan Noodles 34

Lunch Box Noodles 35

Hawaiian Ramen Skillet 36

Sweet Ramen with Tofu 37

Ginger Beef Ramen 38

Ramen Roulade 39

Ramen Lasagna 40

$3 Dollar Dinner 41

Sunflower Ramen with Vinaigrette 42

Cream of Ramen and Mushroom Soup 43

Saucy Serrano Ramen Salad 44

American Ground Beef Ramen 45

Kimchee Noodles 46

Faux Pepperoni Ramen Pizza 47

Roasted Miso Noodles 48

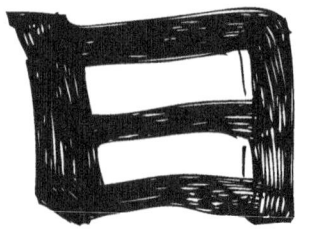

Salad from Vietnam 49

Fried Ramen Rings 50

Thai Ramen Beef Satay 51

Creamy Nuts and Noodles Salad 52

Mock Ramen Pot Pie 53

Tropical Curry Ramen 54

Golden Cheddar Ramen Soup 55

Hot Shot of Ramen 56

Alternative Egg Drop Soup 57

Minty Noodles Cookies 58

Sesame and Chicken Soup 59

Saucy Shrimp and Noodles Chili 60

Instant Spring Noodles 61

Ramen Lunch Special 62

Cashew Stir Fry 63

Toasted Red Wine and Ramen Salad 64

Italian Ramen Skillet 65

Ramen Broccoli Cream Soup 66

Sunny Chicken Coleslaw 67

Hot Apple Ramen Salad 68

Hot Spinach Bowls 69

Irish Ramen Pot Pie 70

Alternative Canadian Poutine 71

Easy Pad Thai Noodles 72

Wavy Tuna Noodles 73

Curry Coleslaw Ramen 74

Healing Black Ramen Broth 75

Curry Coleslaw Ramen 76

Chinese House Ramen 77

Ramen Kyoto 78

Ramen Seafood Soup 79

Florets Bunch Ramen 80

Japanese Restaurant Ramen 81

Akari's Favorite 82

Ramen for 2 83

Milanese Casserole 84

Monterey Ramen 85

Ramen Sake 86

Japanese Ramen Burgers 87

Ramen Summer Salad with Soy Sauce Vinaigrette 88

Enoki Soup 89

Japanese Risotto 90

Hot Ramen Spread 91

Skinny Girl Cabbage Salad 92

Sesame Land 93

Balsamic Golden Noodles 94

Sendai Salad 95

Chicken Breasts Soup on a Ramen Beach 96

Kimchi and Sausage Ramen 97

Syrian Inspired Ramen with Grape Leaves 98

July's Chicken Salad 99

Southwest Ramen Casserole 100

Ramen On Fire 101

Ramen Salad Bowl 102

Ramen in College II 103

4-Ingredient Ramen

Prep Time: 5 mins
Total Time: 10 mins

Servings per Recipe: 2
Calories   306.7
Fat   19.2g
Cholesterol   34.8mg
Sodium   989.2mg
Carbohydrates   28.4g
Protein   5.5g

Ingredients

1 (3 oz.) packages ramen noodles, any flavor
2 C. water
2 tbsp butter
1/4 C. milk

Directions

1. Place a pot over medium heat and fill most of it with water. Cook it until it starts boiling.
2. Stir in it the noodles and let it cook for 4 min. discard the water and place the noodles in an empty pot.
3. Stir in it the milk with butter and seasoning mix. Cook them for 3 to 5 min over low heat until they become creamy. Serve it warm.
4. Enjoy.

MUNG BANG
Noodles Skillet

🥣 Prep Time: 45 mins
🕐 Total Time: 1 hr

Servings per Recipe: 6
Calories 378.5
Fat 16.0g
Cholesterol 54.5mg
Sodium 1082.0mg
Carbohydrates 36.5g
Protein 23.9g

Ingredients
1 lb lean ground beef, cooked
6 slices turkey bacon, chopped
2 (3 oz.) packages ramen noodles
3 garlic cloves, minced
1 medium red onion, diced
1 medium cabbage, chopped
3 carrots, cut into thin 1 inch strips

1 red bell pepper, cut into bite size pieces
2-4 tbsp light soy sauce
3 C. bean sprouts
light soy sauce, to taste
crushed red pepper flakes

Directions
1. Place a large pan over medium heat.
2. Cook in it the bacon until it becomes crisp. Drain it and place it aside. Keep about 2 tbsp of the bacon grease in the pan.
3. Sauté in it the garlic with onion for 4 min. Stir in 2 tbsp of soy sauce and the carrots.
4. Let them cook for 3 min. Stir in the bell pepper with cabbage and let them cook for an extra 7 min.
5. Cook the noodles according to the manufacturer's directions. Drain it and stir it with a splash of olive oil.
6. Stir the beef, bacon and crushed red pepper flakes into the skillet with the cooked veggies. Let them cook for 4 min while stirring often.
7. Once the time is up, stir the bean sprouts and Ramen noodles into the veggies mix. Let them cook for an extra 3 min while stirring all the time.
8. Serve your noodles skillet warm with some hot sauce.
9. Enjoy.

French Ramen Pan

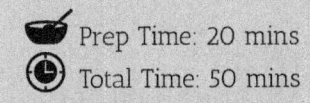

⏱ Prep Time: 20 mins
🕐 Total Time: 50 mins

Servings per Recipe: 1
Calories 540.8
Fat 29.1g
Cholesterol 61.2mg
Sodium 1928.8mg
Carbohydrates 45.9g
Protein 23.2g

Ingredients

- 2 (3 oz.) packages ramen noodles, any flavor
- 2 tbsp sour cream
- 1 (10 1/2 oz.) cans cream of mushroom soup
- 1/2 C. water
- 1/2 C. milk
- 1/4 C. onion, chopped
- 1/4 C. French's French fried onions
- 1/2 lb ground beef

Directions

1. Before you do anything, preheat the oven to 375 F.
2. Get a mixing bowl: Stir in it the crusted noodles, 1 packet of seasoning, sour cream, soup (undiluted) water, milk, and onion.
3. Place a large pan over medium heat. Cook in it the beef for 8 min. Drain it and add it to the noodles mix. Stir them to coat.
4. Pour the mix into a greased pan. Cook it in the oven for 22 min.
5. Top the noodles pan with the fried onion and cook it for an extra 12 min in the oven.
6. Top it with the cheese then serve it warm.
7. Enjoy.

SWEET RAMEN
Skillet

Prep Time: 10 mins
Total Time: 30 mins

Servings per Recipe: 6
Calories 334.3
Fat 11.6g
Cholesterol 48.6mg
Sodium 703.7mg
Carbohydrates 38.0g
Protein 19.9g

Ingredients

1 C. bell pepper, chopped
1/2 tsp ginger
4 whole green onions, thinly sliced
1 (20 oz.) cans pineapple, undrained
1 lb boneless chicken breast
oil
2 (3 oz.) packages chicken-flavored ramen noodles
1/2 C. sweet and sour sauce

Directions

1. Pour the pineapple juice in a measuring C. Stir in it enough water to make 2 C. of liquid in total.
2. Slice the chicken breast into 1 inch dices. Sprinkle over them ginger, a pinch of salt and pepper.
3. Place a large pan over medium heat. Heat a splash of oil in it. Stir in the ramen's seasoning packets and cook them for 30 sec.
4. Stir the pineapple liquid mix into the pan with noodles after cutting into pieces.
5. Cook the mix until it starts boiling. Lower the heat and cook them for 4 min.
6. Once the time is up, stir sweet and sour sauce, pepper, onion, and pineapple into the pan. Let them cook for 4 to 6 min or until the veggies are done.
7. Serve your sweet ramen skillet warm.
8. Enjoy.

How to Make Miso Ramen

Prep Time: 5 mins
Total Time: 20 mins

Servings per Recipe: 5
Calories	279.8
Fat	12.0g
Cholesterol	8.1mg
Sodium	1397.2mg
Carbohydrates	32.7g
Protein	12.4g

Ingredients

- 2 tsp olive oil
- 1 garlic clove, minced
- 1 tsp fresh ginger, minced
- 2-4 oz. ground turkey
- 5 oz. bean sprouts, rinsed
- 4 oz. cabbage, chopped
- 2-4 oz. carrots, cut into thin strips
- 4 C. low sodium chicken broth
- 1 tsp sugar
- 2 tsp light soy sauce
- 4 tbsp miso
- 2 (3 oz.) packages ramen noodles
- 1/2 tsp sesame oil

Directions

1. Place a large saucepan over medium heat. Heat the oil in it. sauté in it the garlic with ginger and turkey for 8 min until done.
2. Stir in the carrots, bean sprouts and cabbage and cook them for 4 min.
3. Stir in the broth with soy sauce and sugar. Cook them until they start boiling.
4. Turn the heat down and sit the miso into the soup with the sesame oil.
5. Enjoy.

MARINATED Eggs for Ramen

Prep Time: 5 mins
Total Time: 10 mins

Servings per Recipe: 1
Calories   83.1
Fat   5.3g
Cholesterol   211.5mg
Sodium   405.1mg
Carbohydrates   1.4g
Protein   6.9g

Ingredients
6 eggs
1 tbsp rice vinegar
2 tbsp soy sauce
1 tsp sugar
1/2 tsp sesame oil

Directions
1. Place a pot over medium heat. Place in it the eggs and cover them with water. Cook them until they start boiling.
2. Turn off the heat and put on the lid. Let the eggs sit for 10 min.
3. Once the time is up drain the eggs and place them in a bowl. Cover them with some cold water and let them sit for 6 min. Peel them and place them aside.
4. Get a small heavy saucepan: Whisk in it the vinegar, soy sauce, sugar, and sesame oil to make the marinade.
5. Cook them over medium heat until they start boiling. Turn off the heat and place the marinade aside until it becomes warm.
6. Place the eggs in a large mason jar and pour the marinade all over them. Seal it and place it aside to sit for 1 day.
7. Once the time is up, drain the eggs and serve them with your ramen.
8. Enjoy.

Apple Ramen Salad

Prep Time: 15 mins
Total Time: 20 mins

Servings per Recipe: 10
Calories   343.1
Fat   28.5g
Cholesterol   9.1mg
Sodium   235.0mg
Carbohydrates   19.8g
Protein   4.0g

Ingredients

12 oz. broccoli florets
1 (12 oz.) bags broccoli coleslaw mix
1/4 C. sunflower seeds
2 (3 oz.) packages ramen noodles
3 tbsp butter
2 tbsp olive oil
1/4 C. sliced almonds

3/4 C. vegetable oil
1/4 C. brown sugar
1/4 C. apple cider vinegar
1/4 C. green onion, chopped

Directions

1. Place a large skillet over medium heat. Heat the oil in it.
2. Press your ramen with your hands to crush it. Stir it in the pan with the almonds.
3. Cook them for 6 min then place the skillet aside.
4. Get a large mixing bowl: Toss in it the broccoli, broccoli slaw and sunflowers. Add the noodles mix and toss them again.
5. Get a small mixing bowl: Combine in it the vegetable oil, brown sugar, apple cider vinegar and the Ramen noodle seasoning packet to make the vinaigrette.
6. Drizzle the vinaigrette all over the salad and stir it to coat. Serve your salad with the green onions on top.
7. Enjoy.

RAMEN
Omelet

Prep Time: 10 mins
Total Time: 25 mins

Servings per Recipe: 6
Calories   247.9
Fat   12.2g
Cholesterol   218.8mg
Sodium   534.9mg
Carbohydrates   21.6g
Protein   12.4g

Ingredients

2 (3 oz.) packages ramen noodles, cooked according to directions
6 eggs
1 red bell pepper, chopped
1 large carrot, grated
1/2 C. parmesan cheese, grated

Directions

1. Get a mixing bowl: Mix in it the eggs with 1 ramen seasoning packet.
2. Add the noodles, bell pepper and carrot. Mix them well.
3. Before you do anything else, preheat the oven to 356 F.
4. Grease a muffin tin with some butter or a cooking spray. Spoon the batter into the tins. Top the muffins with the parmesan cheese.
5. Cook the muffins in the oven for 16 min. Serve them warm.
6. Enjoy.

Ramen Seoul

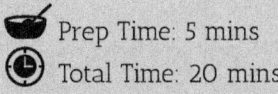

Prep Time: 5 mins
Total Time: 20 mins

Servings per Recipe: 2
Calories   303.0
Fat   9.1g14%
Cholesterol   93.0mg
Sodium   907.1mg
Carbohydrates   45.7g
Protein   9.7g

Ingredients
1 medium potato
1 package ramen noodles
1 green onion, sliced (optional)
1 large egg, beaten

Directions
1. Discard the potato skin and slice them into small dices.
2. Prepare the noodles according to the directions on the package while adding the potato to it and adding 1/4 of the water needed to the pot.
3. Stir the seasoning packet and cook them for potato until it becomes soft.
4. Combine the green onion into the pot and cook them until the ramen is done. Add the eggs to the soup while stirring all the time until they are cooked.
5. Serve your soup hot.
6. Enjoy.

RAMEN
Toscano

Prep Time: 25 mins
Total Time: 60 mins

Servings per Recipe: 4
Calories	611.7
Fat	36.9g
Cholesterol	233.6mg
Sodium	1256.4mg
Carbohydrates	51.4g
Protein	20.2g

Ingredients

1/4 C. olive oil
3 (3 oz.) packages ramen noodles, packet removed
1/2 red bell pepper, sliced
1/4 red onion, sliced
1 small carrot, thinly sliced
3 C. broccoli florets
2 tsp garlic, minced
1 tsp basil
4 eggs, beaten
Spice Mix
1/2 C. parmesan cheese, grated

1/2 C. half-and-half cream
1 tbsp oregano
1/2 tsp kosher salt
3/4 tsp paprika
1/4 tsp dry mustard
3/4 tsp ground fennel
3/4 tsp granulated garlic
3/4 tsp granulated onion
1/4 tsp cayenne pepper
1 pinch sugar

Directions

1. Before you do anything, preheat the oven to 400 F.
2. Get a large mixing bowl: Stir in it the seasoning mix with 1/4 C. of olive oil. Toss the red bell pepper, red onion, broccoli florets into the mix.
3. Stir 1 tsp of minced garlic and basil.
4. Before you do anything, preheat the oven to 350 F.
5. Pour the veggies mix into a greased baking sheet. Cook it in the oven for 22 min.
6. Heat 4 quarts of water in a large pot over medium heat. Cook in it the ramen noodles for 3 to 4 min. Remove the noodles from the water.
7. Get a large mixing bowl: Combine in it the beaten egg, minced garlic, grated Parmesan cheese. Add the noodles and toss them to coat with a pinch of salt and pepper.
8. Grease a casserole dish with some butter. Pour the noodles mix in it and spread it in the pan to make the crust.
9. Spread the baked veggies over the ramen crust.
10. Get a small mixing bowl: Combine in it 3 eggs, the remaining 1/4 C. Parmesan cheese, and 1/2 C. of half and half cream. Mix them well.
11. Drizzle the mix all over the veggies. Cover the pie with a piece of foil. Cook it in the oven for 22 min.
12. Once the time is up, discard the foil. Sprinkle the remaining cheese on top and cook the pie for an extra 12 min.
13. Serve it warm.
14. Enjoy.

Sambal Ramen Salad

Prep Time: 5 mins
Total Time: 7 mins

Servings per Recipe: 2
Calories 425.7
Fat 23.8g
Cholesterol 5.7mg
Sodium 706.6mg
Carbohydrates 46.2g
Protein 10.4g

Ingredients

- 1 (3 oz.) packages ramen noodles
- 1 C. cabbage, shredded
- 4 scallions, cut into 1 inch pieces
- 2-3 carrots
- snow peas, julienned
- 3 tbsp mayonnaise
- 1/2 tsp sambal oelek, or sriracha
- 1-2 tsp lemon juice
- 1/4 C. peanuts, chopped
- cilantro, chopped

Directions

1. Prepare the noodles according to the instructions on the package and cook it for 2 min. Remove it from the water and place it aside to drain.
2. Get a small mixing bowl: Whisk in it the mayo, sambal olek, and lemon juice to make the sauce
3. Get a large mixing bowl: Combine in it the cabbage, carrots, scallions, snow peas, cooked noodles, mayo sauce, a pinch of salt and pepper. Mix them well.
4. Serve your salad and enjoy.

CHILI RAMEN
Casserole

Prep Time: 5 mins
Total Time: 20 mins

Servings per Recipe: 4
Calories	502.3
Fat	24.1g
Cholesterol	54.2mg
Sodium	1979.9mg
Carbohydrates	55.0g
Protein	21.4g

Ingredients

3 packages ramen noodles
2 (15 oz.) cans chili with beans
1 (15 oz.) cans diced tomatoes
4 - 8 oz. shredded cheese

Directions

1. Pour 6 C. of water in a 3 quarts baking pan. Put on the lid and place it in the microwave for 3 to 4 min to heat up.
2. Use a rolling pan to crush the ramen slightly. Stir the noodles into the hot water of in the casserole.
3. Put on the lid and let it cook in the microwave for 2 min 30 sec. Stir the noodles and cook it for an extra 2 min 30 sec.
4. Discard the excess water from the casserole leaving the noodles in it. Add the tomatoes with chili and stir them well.
5. Cook them in the microwave on high for an extra 5 min. Top the ramen casserole with the shredded cheese.
6. Put on the lid and let it sit for several minutes until the cheese melts. Serve your casserole warm.
7. Enjoy.

Broccoli and Oyster Ramen

🥣 Prep Time: 20 mins
🕐 Total Time: 40 mins

Servings per Recipe: 4
Calories   575.7
Fat   32.8g
Cholesterol   75.9mg
Sodium   1207.9mg
Carbohydrates   41.4g
Protein   29.7g

Ingredients

- 1 lb boneless beef top sirloin steak
- 1 tbsp soy sauce
- 1 tbsp apple juice
- 2 tsp cornstarch
- 2 (3 oz.) packages beef-flavor ramen noodles
- 4 C. boiling water
- 2 tbsp olive oil
- 1 onion, chopped
- 3 C. frozen broccoli florets, thawed and drained
- 3 tbsp oyster sauce
- 1 tbsp cornstarch

Directions

1. Place the steak in the freezer until it is partially frozen then thinly slice it.
2. Get a large mixing bowl: Whisk in it the soy sauce, apple juice and 2 tsp cornstarch. Stir the beef into the mix.
3. Get a large mixing bowl: Crush the noodles into pieces stir it in it with the 1 seasoning packet.
4. Add 4 C. of water to the bowl and stir them. Cover the bowl and place it aside.
5. Place a large pan over high heat. Heat the oil in it. Sauté in it the beef for 3 min. Stir in the broccoli and cook it for 4 min.
6. Stir the beef into the skillet and cook them for 8 to 12 min.
7. Get a small mixing bowl: Whisk in it 1 C. of the ramen soaking liquid, oyster sauce, and 1 tbsp cornstarch.
8. Remove the noodles from the water and stir it into the skillet with oyster mix. Cook them until the ramen skillet thickens. Serve it warm.
9. Enjoy.

BABY
Ramen Soup

Prep Time: 15 mins
Total Time: 20 mins

Servings per Recipe: 4
Calories 284.9
Fat 13.3g
Cholesterol 201.2mg
Sodium 1838.1mg
Carbohydrates 19.3g
Protein 20.9g

Ingredients
2 (14 1/2 oz.) cans chicken broth
1/2 lb baby bok choy, halved lengthwise
2 green onions, cut into 2-inch lengths
fresh ginger, minced
1 garlic clove, minced
1 1/2 tsp soy sauce
1 (3 1/2 oz.) packages ramen noodles

1/4 lb sliced ham
4 hard-boiled eggs, peeled and quartered
1 tsp sesame oil

Directions
1. Place a pot over medium heat. Stir in it the broth, bok choy, green onions, ginger, garlic and soy sauce. Simmer them for 12 min.
2. Add the noodles to the pot. Let the soup cook for an extra 4 min.
3. Serve your soup warm with your favorite toppings.
4. Enjoy.

Shoyu Ramen

Prep Time: 10 mins
Total Time: 15 mins

Servings per Recipe: 2
Calories   787.2
Fat   30.0g
Cholesterol   68.4mg
Sodium   4837.8mg
Carbohydrates   89.7g
Protein   41.9g

Ingredients

- 2 boneless skinless chicken breasts
- 2 tbsp sesame oil
- 3 tbsp shoyu
- 1 tbsp rice vinegar
- 1 garlic clove, minced
- 2 tsp honey
- 2 (3 oz.) packages ramen noodles
- 1/3 C. shoyu
- 1/3 C. rice vinegar, unseasoned
- 2 tsp ground ginger
- 2 tbsp honey
- 1 piece konbu
- 1 C. frozen broccoli

Directions

1. Slice the chicken breasts into bite size pieces.
2. Place a large pan over medium heat. Heat 3 tbsp the sesame oil with 3 tbsp shoyu, 1 tbsp of the vinegar, 1 clove of garlic, and 2 tsp of honey. Stir them until they are heated though.
3. Stir the chicken into the pan. Cook it for 6 to 8 min or until it is done.
4. Place a large saucepan over medium heat. Stir in it the remaining shoyu, vinegar, ginger, and honey. Stir enough water that can cover the noodles.
5. Heat them though until they honey melts. Add the veggies with konbu and bring them to a boil.
6. Once the time is up, discard the konbu and stir in the noodles. Cook them for 4 min. Spoon the ramen into serving bowls.
7. Top it with the sweet chicken and serve it warm.
8. Enjoy.

RAMEN
Green Bean Stir Fry

Prep Time: 7 mins
Total Time: 27 mins

Servings per Recipe: 6
Calories   370.9
Fat   27.2g
Cholesterol   0.0mg
Sodium   338.3mg
Carbohydrates   28.2g
Protein   6.4g

Ingredients

1 1/2 lbs fresh green beans
2 (3 oz.) packages ramen noodles
1/2 C. vegetable oil
1/3 C. toasted almond
salt, as needed
black pepper, as needed

Directions

1. Trim the green beans and slice them into 3 to 4 inches pieces.
2. Place the green beans in a steamer and cook them until they become soft.
3. Get a large skillet. Stir in it the oil with 1 seasoning packet.
4. Crush 1 packet of noodles and stir it into the skillet. Add the steamed green beans and cook them for 3 to 4 min.
5. Adjust the seasoning of your stir fry then serve it warm.
6. Enjoy.

Mandarin Ramen Salad

Prep Time: 15 mins
Total Time: 15 mins

Servings per Recipe: 6
Calories   697.2
Fat   50.1g
Cholesterol   0.0mg
Sodium   606.5mg
Carbohydrates   56.0g
Protein   12.1g

Ingredients

1 (16 oz.) packages coleslaw mix
2 (3 oz.) packages ramen noodles, crumbled
1 C. sliced almonds
1 (11 oz.) cans mandarin oranges, drained
1 C. roasted sunflower seeds, shelled
1 bunch green onion, chopped

1/2 C. sugar
3/4 C. vegetable oil
1/3 C. white vinegar
2 packets packet ramen seasoning

Directions

1. Get a small mixing bowl: Whisk in it the vinegar, ramen seasoning, oil and sugar to make the dressing.
2. Get a large mixing bowl: Toss in it the coleslaw mix with noodles, almonds, mandarin, sunflower seeds, and onion.
3. Drizzle the dressing over them and toss them to coat. Place the salad in the fridge for 60 min then serve it.
4. Enjoy.

CHILI
Coconut Ramen

Prep Time: 5 mins
Total Time: 10 mins

Servings per Recipe: 1
Calories   622.3
Fat   33.7g
Cholesterol   0.0mg
Sodium   2087.6mg
Carbohydrates   66.4g
Protein   17.5g

Ingredients
1 (3 oz.) packages ramen noodles
2 tbsp peanut butter
1 tsp low sodium soy sauce
1 1/2 tsp chili-garlic sauce
2-3 tbsp hot water
2 tbsp sweetened flaked coconut
Garnish

broccoli floret
peanuts
shredded carrot

Directions
1. Prepare the noodles according to the directions on the package while discarding the seasoning packet.
2. Get a large mixing bowl: Beat in it the peanut butter, half of the seasoning packet, soy sauce, chili-garlic sauce, 2-3 tbsp of hot water until they become smooth.
3. Add the noodles to the bowl and toss them to coat. Serve your noodles.
4. Enjoy.

Teriyaki Ramen Bowls

Prep Time: 1 hr 30 mins
Total Time: 2 hr

Servings per Recipe: 6
Calories   433.0
Fat   5.6g
Cholesterol   59.8mg
Sodium   2716.9mg
Carbohydrates   63.0g
Protein   36.5g

Ingredients

- 1 1/2 lbs salmon fillets, skinned and boned
- salt & black pepper
- 5 tbsp teriyaki marinade
- vegetable oil, for rubbing
- 2 tbsp red wine vinegar
- 1/4 C. sweet chili sauce
- 6 tbsp Asian fish sauce
- 3 tbsp fresh ginger, grated
- 1 lb soba noodles
- 1 tbsp instant bouillon granules
- 1/2 C. scallion, thinly sliced
- 1 1/2 C. Spinach
- 1 tbsp sesame seeds, toasted

Directions

1. Sprinkle some salt and pepper over the salmon fillets.
2. Get a large zip lock bag: Combine in it the salmon fillets with the teriyaki marinade. Seal the bag and shake it to coat.
3. To make the chili sauce:
4. Get a small mixing bowl: Mix in it the vinegar, chili sauce, fish sauce and ginger. Place it aside.
5. Prepare the noodles according to the directions on the package without the seasoning packet.
6. Remove the salmon fillets from the marinade and coat them with some oil.
7. Place a large pan over medium heat and heat it though. Cook in it the salmon fillet for 3 to 4 min on each side.
8. Add half of the salmon marinade to the pan and coat them with it. Place them aside to sit for 6 min.
9. Cut the salmon into chunks then add to it the spinach with a pinch of salt and pepper. Cook them for 2 to 3 min.
10. Place a large saucepan over medium heat. Cook 6 C. of water in it until they start boiling. Add to it the bouillon powder and the white scallion pieces.
11. Reduce the heat and place the pot aside to make the broth.
12. Drain the noodles and place it in serving bowls. Pour over it the hot broth then top it with the salmon fillets.
13. Enjoy.

RAMEN Steak Skillet

Prep Time: 10 mins
Total Time: 25 mins

Servings per Recipe: 4
Calories 178.8
Fat 8.3g
Cholesterol 0.0mg
Sodium 732.3mg
Carbohydrates 22.1g
Protein 6.0g

Ingredients

1 lb beef round tip steak, stripped
2 cloves garlic, minced
1 tbsp light sesame oil
1/4 tsp ground red pepper
1 (3 oz.) packages ramen noodles
1 (1 lb) package broccoli, carrots and water chestnuts

1 tsp light sesame oil
1 (4 1/2 oz.) jars mushrooms, drained
1 tbsp soy sauce

Directions

1. Get a mixing bowl: Stir in it the beef strips, garlic, one tbsp sesame oil and ground red pepper.
2. Place a pot over medium heat. Cook in it 2 C. of water until it starts boiling. Crush the noodles into 3 portions.
3. Stir it in the pot with the veggies and cook them until they start boiling. Lower the heat and cook them for an extra 3 min.
4. Pour the mix in a colander to remove the water. Place the noodles and veggies mix back into the pot.
5. Add the seasoning packet and stir them well.
6. Place a large pan over medium heat. Heat 1 tsp of sesame oil in it. Cook in it the beef slices for 4 to 5 min or until they are done.
7. Stir the ramen and veggies mix into the skillet with the mushrooms and soy sauce. Cook them for an extra 3 min. Serve your skillet warm.
8. Enjoy.

Parmesan Tuna Ramen

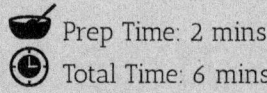
Prep Time: 2 mins
Total Time: 6 mins

Servings per Recipe: 1
Calories   712.6
Fat   31.2g
Cholesterol   106.3mg
Sodium   2590.7mg
Carbohydrates   54.2g
Protein   51.2g

Ingredients

- 1 (3 oz.) packages chicken-flavored ramen noodles
- 1 1/2 C. water
- 1 (6 oz.) canned tuna
- 1-3 tbsp parmesan cheese
- 1 tbsp butter
- parsley flakes
- black pepper

Directions

1. Get a large serving bowl: Pour in it the water.
2. Crush the noodles and add it to the water with the seasoning packet.
3. Place it in the microwave and cook it for 5 min.
4. Stir in the Tuna, Parmesan, Butter, Pepper. Serve it hot.
5. Enjoy.

RAMEN
Sesame Soup

Prep Time: 20 mins
Total Time: 45 mins

Servings per Recipe: 4
Calories 467.9
Fat 21.3g
Cholesterol 78.2mg
Sodium 1630.6mg
Carbohydrates 35.4g
Protein 33.3g

Ingredients
- 1 lb top round steak, julienne
- 1 tbsp peanut oil
- 1/2 tbsp sesame oil
- 1 inch fresh ginger, finely grated
- 2 cloves garlic, minced
- 1/4-1/2 tsp crushed red pepper flakes
- 3 C. beef stock
- 2 bunches scallions, diced
- 2 tbsp rice wine vinegar
- 2 (3 oz.) packets ramen noodles, packet removed
- 1/2 C. baby carrots, grated

Directions
1. Place a large skillet over medium heat. Heat in it 1/3 of each of the oils.
2. Sauté in it the ginger, garlic and red chilies. Cook them for 1 min. Stir in 1/3 of the beef slices. Cook them for 4 min. Place the mix aside.
3. Repeat the process with the remaining beef and oil until it is done.
4. Place a large saucepan over medium heat. Stir in it the Stock, Vinegar,& Scallions. Cook them until they start boiling.
5. Lower the heat and cook it until it starts boiling. Stir in the ramen and cook it for 4 to 4 min or until it is done.
6. Spoon the noodles into serving bowl then top it with the sautéed beef. Serve it warm.
7. Enjoy.

Sweet and Spicy Ramen Stir Fry

Prep Time: 10 mins
Total Time: 30 mins

Servings per Recipe: 4
Calories   585.2
Fat   25.9 g
Cholesterol   0.0 mg
Sodium   2516.7 mg
Carbohydrates   67.4 g
Protein   25.1 g

Ingredients

- 1 (14 oz.) packages extra firm tofu, cubed
- 8 tsp soy sauce
- 2 tbsp vegetable oil
- 8 oz. shiitake mushrooms, sliced thin
- 2 tsp Asian chili sauce
- 3 garlic cloves, minced
- 1 tbsp grated fresh ginger
- 3 1/2 C. low sodium chicken broth
- 4 (3 oz.) packages ramen noodles, packets discarded
- 3 tbsp cider vinegar
- 2 tsp sugar
- 1 (6 oz.) bags Baby Spinach

Directions

1. Use some paper towels to pat the tofu dry.
2. Get a mixing bowl: Stir in it the tofu with 2 tsp of soy sauce.
3. Place a large pan over medium heat. Heat 1 tbsp of oil in it. Sauté in it the tofu for 2 to 3 min on each side then drain it and place it aside.
4. Heat the rest of the oil in the same skillet. Sauté in it the mushroom for 5 min. Add the chili sauce, garlic, and ginger. Let them cook for 40 sec.
5. Crush the ramen into pieces. Stir it into the pan with the broth and cook them for 3 min or until the ramen is done.
6. Add 2 tbsp soy sauce, vinegar, and sugar. Add the spinach and cook them for 2 to 3 min or until it welts.
7. Fold the tofu into the noodles then serve it warm.
8. Enjoy.

LEMONGRASS RAMEN with Duck and Ginger

Prep Time: 10 mins
Total Time: 45 mins

Servings per Recipe: 4
Calories   282.7
Fat   9.4g
Cholesterol   7.2mg
Sodium   789.1mg
Carbohydrates   39.4g
Protein   10.5g

Ingredients

5 C. water
4 C. chicken stock
2 red chilies, seeded and halved
8 slices ginger
3 tbsp lemon juice
3 stalks lemongrass
2 sprigs coriander
1 Chinese barbecued duck, deboned and chopped

4 shallots, chopped
150 g dried ramen noodles
bean sprouts, to garnish
red chile, to garnish
coriander, to garnish
3 bunches bok choy
salt
white pepper

Directions

1. Place a large saucepan over medium heat. Stir in it the water with stock and bring them to a simmer.
2. Crush the lemongrass with coriander and add them to the pot with the galangal, chilis and lime juice. Let them cook for 22 min.
3. Once the time is up, pour the mix in a colander and drain it. Stir the drained mix aside.
4. Add the drain liquid to the saucepan. Stir in the shallot with the duck and cook for 5 min.
5. Prepare the noodles according to the directions on the package without the seasoning packet. Stir the bok choy into the soup and let it cook for an extra 6 min.
6. Serve your soup hot with your favorite toppings.
7. Enjoy.

Creole Ramen

Prep Time: 10 mins
Total Time: 15 mins

Servings per Recipe: 1
Calories   150.2
Fat   12.2g
Cholesterol   94.3mg
Sodium   206.4mg
Carbohydrates   1.2g
Protein   8.8g

Ingredients

1 (3 oz.) packages shrimp flavor ramen noodle soup
6 large shrimp, skin and veins removed
1 tbsp butter
1/4 tsp garlic powder
1 tsp creole seasoning
1/4 tsp black pepper
1/2 tsp hot sauce

Directions

1. Cut the noodles in half and prepare it according to the directions on the package without the seasoning packet.
2. Place a large skillet over medium heat. Melt the butter in it. Sauté in it the shrimp with garlic powder, creole seasoning, and black pepper for 6 min.
3. Pour the noodles with 1/4 C. of the cooking liquid in a serving bowl.
4. Top it with the shrimp and hot sauce then serve it warm.
5. Enjoy.

FERMENTED
Sichuan Noodles

Prep Time: 10 mins
Total Time: 30 mins

Servings per Recipe: 2
Calories 1012.6
Fat 51.7g
Cholesterol 51.7mg
Sodium 3044.3mg
Carbohydrates 92.8g
Protein 46.4g

Ingredients
Sauce
1/2 tbsp fermented black beans
2 tbsp chili bean paste
1/2 tbsp Shaoxing wine or 1/2 tbsp dry sherry
1 tsp soy sauce
1 tsp sesame oil
1 tsp sugar
1/2 tsp ground Sichuan pepper
Noodles

1 tbsp peanut oil or 1 tbsp vegetable oil
4 oz. ground beef
2 scallions, white green parts separated chopped
1 garlic clove, minced
1 tsp fresh ginger, minced
3 C. chicken stock
1 lb tofu, cubes
2 (4 oz.) packages ramen noodles, packet removed

Directions
1. Get a small mixing bowl: Crush in it the black beans with chili bean paste, rice wine, soy sauce, sesame oil, sugar, and Sichuan pepper until they become smooth.
2. Place a large pan over medium heat. Heat the oil in it. Brown in it the beef for 5 min or until done.
3. Stir in the scallion whites, garlic, and ginger and cook them for 1 min over low heat.
4. Stir in the black bean mix with the broth into the pan. Cook them until they start boiling. Lower the heat and stir in the tofu. Let them cook for 6 min.
5. Prepare the noodles according to the directions on the package. Spoon it into serving bowls and top it with tofu mix.
6. Serve your noodles bowels hot.
7. Enjoy.

Lunch Box Noodles

Prep Time: 5 mins
Total Time: 10 mins

Servings per Recipe: 1
Calories   564.1
Fat   27.7g
Cholesterol   34.9mg
Sodium   1225.5mg
Carbohydrates   65.7g
Protein   13.7g

Ingredients

1 (3 oz.) packages ramen noodles
1/2 C. frozen peas
1 tbsp butter
1 tbsp parmesan cheese

Directions

1. Bring a large saucepan of water to a boil. Crush the noodles and stir it into the hot water with the peas.
2. Cook them until they start boiling. Pour the mix in a colander and discard the water.
3. Get a mixing bowl: Toss in it the hot noodles mix with the butter, parmesan, and 1/3 of the ramen's seasoning packet.
4. Serve your noodles bowls warm.
5. Enjoy.

HAWAIIAN
Ramen Skillet

Prep Time: 25 mins
Total Time: 35 mins

Servings per Recipe: 2
Calories	552.7
Fat	38.0g
Cholesterol	61.3mg
Sodium	1944.2mg
Carbohydrates	37.8g
Protein	16.0g

Ingredients
6 oz. turkey spam
1 green bell pepper, stir fried, chopped
1/2 C. onion, diced
1 (3 oz.) packages ramen noodles
1 clove garlic, peeled and diced
1/4 tsp salt
1/4 tsp ground black pepper
1 tbsp olive oil
1/2 tsp butter

Directions
1. Place a large saucepan over medium heat. Cook in it 2 C. of water until they start boiling.
2. Place in it the noodles without the seasoning packet according to the directions on the package. Drain it and place it aside.
3. Place a large skillet over medium heat. Heat in it the butter until it melts with olive oil. Cook in them the onion for 3 min.
4. Stir in the Spam, bell pepper, and the garlic. Cook them for 4 min.
5. Stir in 1/2 C. of the noodles cooking liquid with the drained noodles. Let it sit for 1 min then serve it warm.
6. Enjoy.

Sweet Ramen with Tofu

Prep Time: 10 mins
Total Time: 20 mins

Servings per Recipe: 1
Calories   335.1
Fat   27.8g
Cholesterol   0.0mg
Sodium   33.9mg
Carbohydrates   18.9g
Protein   8.4g

Ingredients

1 package chicken-flavored ramen noodles
2 C. water
2 tbsp vegetable oil
3 slices tofu, 1/4 inch thick
2 C. soy bean sprouts or 2 C. mung bean sprouts
1/2 small zucchini, thinly sliced
2 green onions, sliced
1/2 C. sweet green pea pods
flour
seasoning salt
sesame oil

Directions

1. Slice each tofu piece into 3 chunks. Dust them with some flour.
2. Place a large skillet over medium heat. Heat 1 tbsp of oil in it. Cook in it the tofu for 1 to 2 min on each side. Drain it and place it aside.
3. Heat a splash of oil in the same pan. Sauté in it the veggies for 6 min. Place them aside.
4. Cook the noodles by following the directions on the package. Stir in it the seasoning packet.
5. Place a large skillet over medium heat. Heat a splash of oil in it. Cook in it the bean sprouts for 1 min.
6. Lay the fried bean sprouts in the bottom of serving bowl. Top it with the ramen, cooked veggies and tofu. Serve them hot.
7. Enjoy.

GINGER Beef Ramen

Prep Time: 20 mins
Total Time: 40 mins

Servings per Recipe: 4
Calories   902.3
Fat   42.4g
Cholesterol   68.2mg
Sodium   2750.8mg
Carbohydrates   89.7g
Protein   39.5g

Ingredients

14 oz. dried ramen noodles
12 oz. beef sirloin, half frozen to make slicing easier
1 1/2 quarts chicken stock
1 inch piece gingerroot, roughly sliced
2 garlic cloves, halved
2 tbsp sake
3 tbsp shoyu, plus
1 tbsp shoyu, for stir-frying
1 bok choy, trimmed and thinly shredded

2 tbsp peanut oil
8 dried shiitake mushrooms, soaked in warm water for 30 minutes, drained and thinly sliced
sea salt, to taste
fresh ground black pepper, to taste

Directions

1. Prepare the noodles according to the instructions on the package. Discard the water and place the noodles aside.
2. Slice the beef into thin slices.
3. Place a large saucepan over medium heat. Heat the stock in it. Stir in it the ginger with garlic and cook them for 12 min over low heat.
4. Once the time is up, drain the ginger with garlic and discard them. Add the sake, shoyu and salt and pepper to the broth.
5. Place a large pan over medium heat. Heat 1 tbsp of oil in it. Sauté in it the baby bok choy for 3 min. Drain it and place it aside.
6. Heat the remaining oil in the same skillet. Sauté in it the beef with mushroom for 4 min. Stir into them the shoyu with a pinch of salt and pepper.
7. Stir the noodles in some hot water to heat it then drain it. Place it in serving bowls then top it with the beef, shiitake, and bok choy.
8. Pour the chicken broth all over them. Serve it right away.
9. Enjoy.

Ramen Roulade

Prep Time: 10 mins
Total Time: 55 mins

Servings per Recipe: 6
Calories   268.8
Fat   12.6g
Cholesterol   81.7mg
Sodium   238.6mg
Carbohydrates   10.4g
Protein   26.5g

Ingredients

- 1 1/2 lbs flank steaks
- 3 tbsp seasoning salt
- pepper
- 1 egg, beaten
- 1 tbsp water
- 1 tbsp flour
- 1 (3 oz.) packages Top Ramen noodles, packet discarded
- toothpick
- 2 tbsp steak sauce

Directions

1. Before you do anything, preheat the oven to 350 F.
2. Place 2 flank steaks on a broad. Flatten them with a kitchen hammer.
3. Season the steak pieces with the McCormick All Seasoning, a pinch of salt and pepper on both sides.
4. Get a small mixing bowl: MIX in it the eggs with water. Add the flour and mix them well.
5. Lather the mix all over 1 side of the steak pieces. Break the ramen into pieces and lay it all over the steak pieces.
6. Roll the steaks over the filling and seal them with toothpicks.
7. Place the steaks roulades on a greased baking sheet. Cook them in the oven for 42 to 46 min.
8. Drizzle the steak sauce over the roulades and cook them for an extra 12 min. allow them to rest for 12 min then serve them with your favorite toppings.
9. Enjoy.

RAMEN
Lasagna

Prep Time: 10 mins
Total Time: 20 mins

Servings per Recipe: 4
Calories	698.6
Fat	41.9g
Cholesterol	253.4mg
Sodium	1670.9mg
Carbohydrates	36.5g
Protein	41.9g

Ingredients
- 2 (3 oz.) packages ramen noodles
- 1 lb ground beef
- 3 eggs
- 2 C. shredded cheese
- 1 tbsp minced onion
- 1 C. spaghetti sauce

Directions
1. Before you do anything preheat the oven to 325 F.
2. Place a large skillet over medium heat. Cook in it the beef with 1 seasoning packet and onion for 10 min.
3. Transfer the beef to a greased baking pan. Whisk the eggs and cook them in the same pan until they are done.
4. Top the beef with 1/2 C. of shredded cheese followed by the cooked eggs and another 1/2 C. of cheese.
5. Cook the ramen noodles according to the instructions on the package. Drain it and toss it with the spaghetti sauce.
6. Spread the mix all over the cheese layer. Top it with the remaining cheese. Cook it in the oven for 12 min. serve your lasagna warm.
7. Enjoy.

$3 Dollar Dinner

Prep Time: 3 mins
Total Time: 5 mins

Servings per Recipe: 1
Calories   780.9
Fat   27.8g
Cholesterol   30.6mg
Sodium   2388.2mg
Carbohydrates   69.2g
Protein   62.3g

Ingredients

1 (6 oz.) cans tuna in vegetable oil
1 (3 oz.) packets ramen noodles, any flavor
1/2 C. frozen mixed vegetables

Directions

1. Place a large skillet over medium heat. Heat in it a splash of oil. Cook in it the tuna for 2 to 3 min.
2. Prepare the ramen noodles according to the directions on the package with the veggies.
3. Remove the noodles and veggies from the water and transfer them to the pan. Stir into them the seasoning packet and cook them for 2 to 3 min.
4. Serve your ramen tuna warm.
5. Enjoy.

SUNFLOWER RAMEN
with Vinaigrette

Prep Time: 10 mins
Total Time: 10 mins

Servings per Recipe: 8
Calories 430.6
Fat 28.9g
Cholesterol 0.0mg
Sodium 777.8mg
Carbohydrates 37.0g
Protein 8.8g

Ingredients

Ramen
16 oz. shredded cabbage, or coleslaw mix
2/3 C. sunflower seeds
1/2 C. slivered almonds
3 bags oriental-flavor instant ramen noodles, crunched, uncooked, packet saved
1 bunch green onion, chopped
Vinaigrette
1/2 C. oil
3 tbsp red wine vinegar
3 tbsp sugar
2 tsp pepper
3 packages seasoning from oriental-flavor instant ramen noodles

Directions

1. Get a large mixing bowl: Toss in it the salad ingredients.
2. Get a small mixing bowl: Whisk in it the dressing ingredients.
3. Drizzle the dressing over the salad and toss them to coat. Serve it right away.
4. Enjoy.

Cream of Ramen and Mushroom Soup

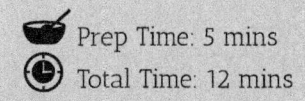

Prep Time: 5 mins
Total Time: 12 mins

Servings per Recipe: 4
Calories 203.3
Fat 11.0g
Cholesterol 15.9mg
Sodium 990.0mg
Carbohydrates 18.6g
Protein 7.4g

Ingredients

1 (3 oz.) packages chicken-flavored ramen noodles
1 (10 3/4 oz.) cans cream of mushroom soup
1 (3 oz.) cans chicken

Directions

1. Prepare the ramen according to the directions on the package.
2. Place a large saucepan over medium heat. Stir in it the soup, chicken and seasoning. Cook them for 6 min.
3. Drain the noodles and divide it between serving bowls. Spoon the soup mix over it then serve it warm.
4. Enjoy.

SAUCY
Serrano Ramen Salad

Prep Time: 10 mins
Total Time: 25 mins

Servings per Recipe: 2
Calories 533.3
Fat 19.5g
Cholesterol 0.3mg
Sodium 1990.6mg
Carbohydrates 77.4g
Protein 13.6g

Ingredients

1 yellow onion, chopped
2 roma tomatoes, chopped
1 serrano chili, chopped
1 red pepper, roasted and peeled, medium chopped
1 C. mixed vegetables diced
2 (3 oz.) packets oriental-flavor instant ramen noodles
1 vegetable bouillon cube
1 tsp cumin powder
1 tsp red chili powder
4 tbsp spaghetti sauce
2 tsp canola oil or 2 tsp any other vegetable oil

Directions

1. Place a large pan over medium heat. Heat the oil in it. Sauté in it the onion with tomato and serrano chili for 3 min.
2. Stir in a seasoning packet and the Maggi bouillon cube. Stir in the veggies, the cumin and 1/2 a C. of water. Cook them for 6 min.
3. Stir in the spaghetti sauce and cook them for an extra 6 min.
4. Prepare the noodles according to the directions on the package. Toss the noodles with the veggies mix. Serve it hot.
5. Enjoy.

American Ground Beef Ramen

Prep Time: 7 mins
Total Time: 12 mins

Servings per Recipe: 4
Calories   770.2
Fat   29.6g
Cholesterol   77.1mg
Sodium   1849.2mg
Carbohydrates   91.2g
Protein   38.7g

Ingredients

1 lb ground beef, drained
3 (3 oz.) packets beef-flavor ramen noodles
5 C. boiling water
1/4-1/2 C. water
1 (16 oz.) cans corn
1 (16 oz.) cans peas
1/4 C. soy sauce
1/2 tsp ground red pepper
1 dash cinnamon
2 tsp sugar

Directions

1. Place a large pan over medium heat. Heat a splash of oil in it. Add the beef and cook it for 8 min. Place it aside.
2. Place a large saucepan over medium heat. Heat 5 C. of water in it until it starts boiling. Cook in it the noodles for 3 to 4 min.
3. Remove the noodles from the water and stir it into the skillet with the beef.
4. Add the water, corn, peas, soy sauce, red pepper, cinnamon, sugar and 1 and a half of the seasoning packets. Toss them to coat.
5. Let them cook for 6 min while stirring often. Serve your ramen Skillet Hot.
6. Enjoy.

KIMCHEE
Noodles

Prep Time: 5 mins
Total Time: 25 mins

Servings per Recipe: 2
Calories	830.8
Fat	66.1g
Cholesterol	117.6mg
Sodium	3186.4mg
Carbohydrates	32.7g
Protein	26.8g

Ingredients
1 1/2 C. kimchee
1 (3 oz.) packages oriental-flavor instant ramen noodles
1 (12 oz.) packages turkey spam, cubed
2 tbsp vegetable oil

Directions
1. Cook the noodles according to the instructions on the package.
2. Place the pan over medium heat. Heat the oil in it. Sauté in it the spam pieces for 3 min.
3. Stir in the noodles after draining it and cook them for an extra 3 min.
4. Stir in the kimchee and cook them for 2 min. serve your noodles warm.
5. Enjoy.

Faux Pepperoni Ramen Pizza

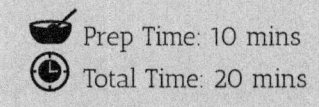

Prep Time: 10 mins
Total Time: 20 mins

Servings per Recipe: 6
Calories 170.6
Fat 7.9g
Cholesterol 17.4mg
Sodium 764.5mg
Carbohydrates 17.7g
Protein 7.0g

Ingredients

1 (3 oz.) packages ramen noodles, any flavor
1 tbsp olive oil
1 (14 oz.) jars spaghetti sauce
1 C. low-fat mozzarella cheese, shredded
3 oz. beef pepperoni
1/2 tsp dried oregano

Directions

1. Before you do anything, preheat the oven broiler.
2. Prepare the noodles according to the instructions on the package without the seasoning packet. Drain it.
3. Place a large oven proof pan over medium heat. Heat the oil in it. Sauté in it the noodles and press it to the bottom of it for 2 min to make the crust.
4. Pour the sauce all over the noodles and top it with 2 oz. pepperoni slices. Sprinkle the cheese on top followed by the remaining pepperoni and oregano.
5. Transfer the pan to the oven and cook them for 2 to 3 min or until the cheese melts.
6. Allow your pizza to lose the heat for 6 min. serve it.
7. Enjoy.

ROASTED
Miso Noodles

Prep Time: 30 mins
Total Time: 45 mins

Servings per Recipe: 2
Calories 1069.2
Fat 50.5g
Cholesterol 465.4mg
Sodium 2844.7mg
Carbohydrates 93.7g
Protein 61.8g

Ingredients
4 large eggs, hard boiled
1 tbsp unsalted butter
1 C. sweet corn
1 tbsp olive oil
8 oz. fresh spinach
1 quart chicken stock
1 tsp red miso
6 oz. ramen noodles
6 oz. cooked chicken
4 green onions, thinly sliced

1 tsp toasted sesame oil, for drizzling

Directions
1. Place a small saucepan over medium heat. Melt in it the butter. Add the corn with a pinch of salt and pepper then heat them though. Place it aside.
2. Place a large pan over medium heat. Heat the oil in it. Add to it the spinach and cook them for 2 min. Place it aside.
3. Place a large saucepan over medium heat. Heat in it the chicken stock until it starts boiling. Add to it the miso paste and mix them well.
4. Stir in the noodles and cook it for 3 min. Spoon the noodles into serving bowls.
5. Top it with the corn, spinach and chicken. Garnish it with the green onions, sesame oil and eggs. Serve them hot.
6. Enjoy.

Salad from Vietnam

> Prep Time: 10 mins
> Total Time: 10 mins
>
> Servings per Recipe: 8
> Calories   238.2
> Fat   18.7g
> Cholesterol   0.0mg
> Sodium   526.6mg
> Carbohydrates   15.8g
> Protein   3.7g

Ingredients

- 1/2 head green cabbage, finely chopped
- 4 green onions, finely chopped
- 1/2 bunch fresh curly-leaf parsley
- 2 tbsp sugar
- 1 tsp salt
- 1/2 tsp black pepper
- 1/2 C. olive oil
- 3 tbsp white balsamic vinegar
- 1 (3 oz.) packages chicken-flavored ramen noodles, uncooked
- 2 oz. slivered almonds

Directions

1. Get a large mixing bowl: Toss in it the cabbage, green onions, parsley and coarsely crumbled uncooked ramen noodles.
2. Get a small mixing bowl: Mix in it the sugar, salt, black pepper, olive oil, vinegar, seasoning packet, a pinch of salt and pepper to make the vinaigrette.
3. Add it to the salad and toss them to coat. Place the salad in the fridge for 3 h to an overnight.
4. Sprinkle the almonds on top then serve it.
5. Enjoy.

FRIED
Ramen Rings

🥣 Prep Time: 20 mins
🕒 Total Time: 35 mins

Servings per Recipe: 1
Calories 1490.7
Fat 37.4g
Cholesterol 372.0mg
Sodium 7533.7mg
Carbohydrates 224.1g
Protein 45.5g

Ingredients
Batter for Frying, reserve 2 C.
1 C. self-rising flour
1 tsp salt
1/4 tsp pepper
2 eggs, beaten
1 C. beer, or milk
Onions

2 (3 oz.) packages ramen noodles, packet reserved
oil, for frying
1 large Vidalia onion, ringed

Directions
1. Get a large mixing bowl: Whisk in it the flour, eggs, beer, a pinch of salt and pepper.
2. Get a food processor: Cut the one ramen in half and process it in it until it becomes ground. Add it to the flour batter and mix them well.
3. Finely crush the other ramen and place it in a shallow dish. Add to it the seasoning packet and mix them well.
4. Place a large pan over medium heat. Fill 3/4 inch of it with oil and heat it.
5. Coat the onion rings with the flour batter and dip them in the crushed noodles mix. Place them in the hot oil and cook them until they become golden brown.
6. Serve your onion rings with your favorite dip.
7. Enjoy.

Thai Ramen Beef Satay

Prep Time: 30 mins
Total Time: 38 mins

Servings per Recipe: 4
Calories   794.6
Fat   43.3g
Cholesterol   154.2mg
Sodium   1959.2mg
Carbohydrates   39.6g
Protein   63.0g

Ingredients

Marinade
2 tbsp soy sauce
2 tbsp lime juice
1 1/2 tsp sugar
1 1/2 tsp fresh ginger, grated, peeled
1 garlic clove, grated (optional)
1/4 tsp red pepper flakes (optional)
2 lbs flank steaks, thinly sliced against the grain
Peanut Ramen Glaze
1 tbsp lime juice
1 tsp sugar
1 tsp fresh ginger, grated and peeled
1/3 C. creamy peanut butter
1/3 C. water
1 tbsp soy sauce
1/4 tsp red pepper flakes (optional)
1/4 C. roasted peanuts, chopped
3 green onions, sliced
vegetable oil, for grill
2 (3 oz.) packages ramen noodles, cooked, packet removed

Directions

1. Place 12 wooden skewers in some water and let them sit for 16 min.
2. Get a roasting pan: Mix in it 2 tbsp each soy sauce and lime juice and 1 1/2 tsp each sugar and ginger, garlic and/or 1/4 tsp optional red pepper flakes to make the marinade.
3. Add the beef slices to the marinade and toss them to coat. Place them aside to sit for 12 min.
4. Get a food processor: Combine in it 1 tbsp lime juice, 1 tsp sugar, and 1 tsp ginger with peanut butter and 1/3 C. water. Process them until they become smooth.
5. Add the rest of the soy sauce and process them again. Pour the mix in small mixing bowl.
6. Stir in it the chopped peanuts and green onions and optional remaining 1/4 tsp of red pepper flakes to make the sauce.
7. Before you do anything else preheat the grill and grease it.
8. Drain the beef slices and thread them into the wooden skewers. Cook the beef slices on the grill for 4 to 5 min on each side.
9. Spoon the noodles into serving bowls. Drizzle the peanut sauce over it and top it with the grilled beef. Serve them hot.
10. Enjoy.

CREAMY NUTS and Noodles Salad

Prep Time: 15 mins
Total Time: 20 mins

Servings per Recipe: 4
Calories   318.5
Fat   19.8g
Cholesterol   15.2mg
Sodium   446.3mg
Carbohydrates   33.4g
Protein   4.1g

Ingredients
1 packages chicken-flavored ramen noodles
1 C. diced celery
1 (8 oz.) cans sliced water chestnuts, drained
1 C. chopped red onion
1 C. diced green pepper
1 C. peas
1 C. mayonnaise

Directions
1. Crush the noodles into 4 pieces. Prepare them according to the instructions on the package.
2. Get a large mixing bowl: Drain the noodles and toss it with the celery, water chestnuts, onion, pepper and peas in it.
3. Get a small mixing bowl: Whisk in it the mayo with 3 seasoning packets. Add them to the salad and toss them to coat.
4. Place the salad in the fridge for 1 to 2 h then serve it.
5. Enjoy.

Mock Ramen Pot Pie

Prep Time: 15 mins
Total Time: 30 mins

Servings per Recipe: 4
Calories   528.6
Fat   24.9g
Cholesterol   77.1mg
Sodium   957.3mg
Carbohydrates   49.0g
Protein   29.1g

Ingredients
2 (3 oz.) packages ramen noodles
1 lb ground beef
1 (15 oz.) cans sweet corn
1/2 C. onion, chopped
vegetable oil

Directions
1. Before you do anything preheat the oven to 350 F.
2. Prepare the noodles according to the directions on the package.
3. Place a large pan over medium heat. Heat a splash of oil in it. Cook in it the beef with onion for 12 min.
4. Spread the mix in the bottom of a greased baking pan. Top it with the sweet corn and the ramen noodles after draining it.
5. Place the casserole in the oven and cook it for 14 to 16 min. Serve it warm.
6. Enjoy.

TROPICAL
Curry Ramen

Prep Time: 20 mins
Total Time: 30 mins

Servings per Recipe: 4
Calories 553.2
Fat 25.4g
Cholesterol 0.0mg
Sodium 1466.3mg
Carbohydrates 76.3g
Protein 8.5g

Ingredients

2 (3 oz.) packages ramen noodles
1 tbsp vegetable oil
1 tsp crushed red pepper flakes
2 garlic cloves, minced
1 C. shredded cabbage
1 C. thinly sliced mixed mushrooms
1 C. chopped broccoli
1 tbsp peanut butter
1 tbsp soy sauce
1 tbsp brown sugar
1 C. coconut milk
1 tsp curry powder
1 tsp sambal oelek
1 lime, juice of
1/2 tsp salt
1 tbsp crushed peanuts
1/4 C. chopped cilantro
lime wedge

Directions

1. Prepare the noodles according to the directions on the package without the seasoning packets. Drain the noodles and reserve the cooking liquid.
2. Place a large pan over medium heat. Heat the oil in it. Sauté in it the garlic with red pepper for 40 sec.
3. Stir in the cabbage, mushrooms and broccoli. Add the veggies and cook them for 6 min. Stir the noodles into the pan and place them aside.
4. Place another pan over medium heat. Stir in it the peanut butter, soy sauce, brown sugar, coconut milk, curry powder, sambal oelek and salt. Cook them until they start boiling.
5. Add the cooked noodles and veggies and stir them to coat. Stir in 1/4 C. of the cooking liquid. Cook them until they mix becomes thick.
6. Let the ramen skillet rest for 6 min. Top the ramen skillet with the cilantro and peanuts then serve them hot.
7. Enjoy.

Golden Cheddar Ramen Soup

Prep Time: 2 mins
Total Time: 8 mins

Servings per Recipe: 1
Calories   617.0
Fat   24.4g
Cholesterol   30.6mg
Sodium   1236.9mg
Carbohydrates   85.0g
Protein   17.2g

Ingredients

Ramen
1 (3 oz.) packages ramen noodles
2 C. water
Base
1 seasoning, packet
1-2 C. water

1 tbsp freshly shredded parmesan cheese
1/4 C. shredded aged white cheddar cheese
1/4 C. golden raisins
Tabasco sauce

Directions

1. Stir 2 C. of water and 1 ramen packet in a heatproof bowl. Place it in the microwave for 5 to 7 min.
2. Once the time is up, stir the parmesan and cheddar cheese into the noodles until they melt. Fold the raisins into it and serve it hot.
3. Enjoy.

HOT SHOT
of Ramen

Prep Time: 10 mins
Total Time: 23 mins

Servings per Recipe: 2
Calories   365.6
Fat   15.5g
Cholesterol   47.5mg
Sodium   861.7mg
Carbohydrates   35.0g
Protein   20.8g

Ingredients
1 1/2 C. water
1 small yellow onion, finely diced
1 celery rib, finely diced
6 baby carrots, julienne
1 (3 oz.) packages ramen noodles, broken
1 (5 1/2 oz.) cans sardines in tomato sauce
2-3 dashes hot sauce

Directions
1. Place a large saucepan of water over medium heat. Stir in it the water, onion, celery, and carrots. Cook them for 12 min.
2. Stir in the noodles and cook it for 3 to 4 min.
3. Stir the sardines with tomato, and hot sauce into the saucepan. Serve it hot with your favorite toppings.
4. Enjoy.

Alternative Egg Drop Soup

Prep Time: 15 mins
Total Time: 27 mins

Servings per Recipe: 4
Calories	366.9
Fat	21.7g
Cholesterol	105.8mg
Sodium	489.3mg
Carbohydrates	31.3g
Protein	16.2g

Ingredients

- 3 C. water
- 1 (3 oz.) packages ramen noodles
- 1 vegetarian bouillon cube
- garlic powder
- onion powder
- five-spice powder
- pepper
- 4 oz. peanuts
- 4 oz. frozen broccoli
- 4 oz. frozen cauliflower
- 4 oz. frozen corn
- 4 oz. frozen peas
- 2 large eggs
- 1 tsp toasted sesame oil
- soy sauce or hoisin sauce

Directions

1. Place a pot over medium heat. Cook in 3 C. of water until the start boiling.
2. Stir in the bouillon and spices; noodles, broccoli and cauliflower. Cook them until they start boiling.
3. Stir in the peas with corn and peanut then cook them again until they start boiling. Stir in the eggs into the soup and cook it until it starts boiling again.
4. Stir in the seasoning packet with hoisin sauce, and sesame oil. Serve your soup hot.
5. Enjoy.

MINTY
Noodles Cookies

🥣 Prep Time: 10 mins
🕐 Total Time: 1 hr 10 mins

Servings per Recipe: 24
Calories   155.2
Fat   8.0g
Cholesterol   0.0mg
Sodium   166.5mg
Carbohydrates   21.2g
Protein   2.1g

Ingredients
4 (3 oz.) packets ramen noodles, uncooked
1 (16 oz.) bags dark chocolate chips
12-14 drops peppermint extract
1-2 drop spear mint extract
1-2 drop wintergreen extract
24 lollipop sticks
1/2 tsp butter (optional)

Directions
1. Break the noodles into pieces and place it in a mixing bowl.
2. Place a pot over low heat. Stir in it the chocolate chips with butter until they melt. Stir in the mint extract. Cook them for 1 min.
3. Pour the mix all over the noodles and mix them well.
4. Use a large tbsp to spoon the mix in the shape of cookies on a lined up baking sheet. place the pan in the fridge for at least 1 h.
5. Serve your cookies with your favorite toppings.
6. Enjoy.

Sesame and Chicken Soup

Prep Time: 10 mins
Total Time: 18 mins

Servings per Recipe: 4
Calories 352.8
Fat 10.8g
Cholesterol 72.6mg
Sodium 1036.5mg
Carbohydrates 32.5g
Protein 30.1g

Ingredients
5 C. water
2 (3 oz.) packages chicken-flavored ramen noodles
6 oz. snow peas, cut up diagonally in half
2 green onions, sliced
1 large carrot, shredded
1 lb boneless skinless chicken breast, cut into 3/4 inch pieces
1 tsp sesame oil

Directions
1. Place a large saucepan over medium heat. Heat in it the water until it starts boiling.
2. Stir in the noodles snow peas, green onions, carrot, and chicken. Let them cook for 4 to 6 min over high heat.
3. Turn off the heat and stir the sesame oil into it. Serve it hot.
4. Enjoy.

SAUCY Shrimp and Noodles Chili

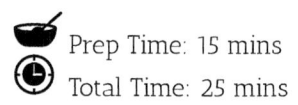

Prep Time: 15 mins
Total Time: 25 mins

Servings per Recipe: 10
Calories   131.9
Fat   1.3g
Cholesterol   69.1mg
Sodium   369.7mg
Carbohydrates   17.8g
Protein   13.7g

Ingredients

1 lb deveined medium shrimp
1 tbsp lemon juice
1/2 tsp chili powder
1/8 tsp cumin
1/8 tsp pepper
3 C. water
2 (3 oz.) packages shrimp flavor ramen noodles
16 oz. salsa

15 oz. black beans, drained and rinsed
2 C. frozen corn
1/4 C. chopped fresh cilantro (optional)

Directions

1. Get a mixing bowl: Whisk in it the lemon juice, chili powder, cumin and pepper. Stir in it the shrimp and place it aside for 22 min.
2. Place a pot over medium heat. Heat in it some water until it starts boiling. Crush the noodles and stir it with 1 seasoning packet.
3. Bring them to a boil and let them cook for 1 min.
4. Stir the shrimp into the soup pot and cook them for 2 min. Add the salsa, beans and corn to the pot. Cook the soup for 6 min. serve it hot.
5. Enjoy.

Instant Spring Noodles

Prep Time: 5 mins
Total Time: 10 mins

Servings per Recipe: 4
Calories   176.3
Fat   4.2g
Cholesterol   0.0mg
Sodium   307.1mg
Carbohydrates   30.7g
Protein   6.1g

Ingredients
1 (3 oz.) packages ramen noodles, any flavor
1 (16 oz.) packages frozen mixed vegetables, the kind you microwave in the bag
1 1/2 C. water

Directions
1. Cook the vegetables in the microwave according to the instructions on the package.
2. Prepare the noodles according to the directions on the package. Stir the veggies with the seasoning packet into the soup.
3. Let it cook for 6 min then serve it hot.
4. Enjoy.

RAMEN
Lunch Special

Prep Time: 10 mins
Total Time: 4 h 10 mins

Servings per Recipe: 12
Calories 318.7
Fat 11.3g
Cholesterol 24.5mg
Sodium 804.7mg
Carbohydrates 41.9g
Protein 14.1g

Ingredients

6 (2 7/8 oz.) packages beef-flavor ramen noodles
1 lb lean ground beef
1 (14 1/2 oz.) cans cut green beans, drained
24 oz. whole kernel corn, drained
2 carrots, diced
3 celery ribs, diced
6 oz. frozen peas
12 C. water

Directions

1. Place a large saucepan over medium heat. Bring 2 C. of water in it to a boil. Cook in it the celery and carrots until they become soft.
2. Place a large pan over medium heat. Cook in it the beef for 10 min. Drain it and place it aside.
3. Cut the ramen into 4 pieces and place them in crock pot. Sprinkle over them the seasoning packet. Stir in the corn with beans and peas after draining them.
4. Pour 10 C. of water all over them. Stir in the cooked beef with celery and carrot and their water.
5. Put on the lid and cook them for 120 min on high.
6. Once the time is up, change the settings to low and cook them for an extra 120 min. Serve your soup hot.
7. Enjoy.

Cashew Stir Fry

🍲 Prep Time: 3 mins
🕐 Total Time: 6 mins

Servings per Recipe: 1
Calories   1321.2
Fat   64.7g
Cholesterol   0.0mg
Sodium   2988.3mg
Carbohydrates   161.0g
Protein   26.7g

Ingredients
- 1 (8 oz.) packages ramen noodles
- 1 tbsp sesame oil
- 1/4 C. chicken broth
- 3 tbsp crushed cashews
- 2 tsp crushed red pepper flakes
- 2 tsp onion flakes

Directions
1. Prepare the noodles according to the directions on the package.
2. Place a large pan over medium heat. Heat the oil in it. Stir in it the heat oil, broth, cashews, pepper, half the seasoning packet and onion flakes.
3. Drain the noodles and add it to the pan. Cook them for 1 min then serve your stir fry hot.
4. Enjoy.

TOASTED Red Wine and Ramen Salad

Prep Time: 10 mins
Total Time: 13 mins

Servings per Recipe: 4
Calories   868.7
Fat   71.7g
Cholesterol   0.0mg
Sodium   1782.6mg
Carbohydrates   48.1g
Protein   17.3g

Ingredients

1 cabbage, medium head shredded
2 green onions, minced
5 5/8 oz. ramen noodles
3/4 C. sunflower oil
6 tbsp red wine vinegar
2 tsp salt
1/2 tsp pepper
5 tbsp sunflower seeds, hulled
1 C. almonds, toasted slivered

Directions

1. Get a large mixing bowl: Toss in it the green onion with cabbage. Put on the lid and place it in the fridge.
2. Get a mixing bowl: Whisk in it the seasoning packet with oil, vinegar, salt and pepper to make the dressing.
3. Break the noodles into pieces and add it to the salad with the dressing, sunflower seeds and almonds. Serve your salad right away and enjoy.

Italian Ramen Skillet

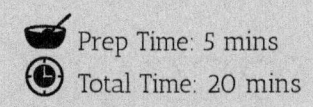

🍜 Prep Time: 5 mins
🕐 Total Time: 20 mins

Servings per Recipe: 1
Calories   439.1
Fat   23.7g
Cholesterol   77.1mg
Sodium   955.0mg
Carbohydrates   29.1g
Protein   25.7g

Ingredients

2 (3 oz.) packages beef-flavor ramen noodles
1 lb ground beef
1/2 C. chopped onion
1 (11 1/8 oz.) cans condensed Italian tomato soup
water, 1/2 soup can
1 tsp Worcestershire sauce

1 tsp prepared mustard
generous dash pepper
fresh basil leaf
fresh oregano sprig
tomatoes, slices and
grated parmesan cheese, for garnish

Directions

1. Prepare the noodles according to the directions on the package. Discard the water. Stir the seasoning packet into the noodles.
2. Place a large pan over medium heat. Sauté in it the onion with beef for 8 min. Drain it and discard the fat.
3. Add the tomato soup, water, Worcestershire sauce, cooked noodles, mustard and pepper and stir them well. Cook them for 5 min.
4. Serve your noodles skillet hot with your favorite toppings.
5. Enjoy.

RAMEN
Broccoli Cream Soup

Prep Time: 10 mins
Total Time: 25 mins

Servings per Recipe: 6
Calories   202.6
Fat   9.4g
Cholesterol   13.2mg
Sodium   729.9mg
Carbohydrates   24.2g
Protein   5.7g

Ingredients

4 C. water
2 (3 oz.) packages chicken flavored ramen noodles
1 1/2 C. broccoli florets
1 (11 oz.) cans condensed soup, cheddar cheese
1/4 C. plain yogurt
1/8 tsp pepper

Directions

1. Place a large saucepan over medium heat. Cook in it 3 quarts water until it starts boiling.
2. Add the noodles with broccoli and bring them to a boil. Lower the heat and put on the lid then cook for 6 min.
3. Add 1 seasoning packet to the saucepan followed by the cheese soup, sour cream and pepper. Cook them for an extra 3 min.
4. Adjust the seasoning of the soup then serve it hot.
5. Enjoy.

Sunny Chicken Coleslaw

Prep Time: 15 mins
Total Time: 22 mins

Servings per Recipe: 4
Calories 730.7
Fat 52.8g
Cholesterol 68.5mg
Sodium 523.7mg
Carbohydrates 33.1g
Protein 34.5g

Ingredients

- 1 (3 oz.) packages oriental-flavor instant ramen noodles
- 1/2 C. slivered almonds
- 1/2 C. sunflower seeds
- 1/2 C. vegetable oil
- 2 tbsp sugar
- 2 tbsp cider vinegar
- 2 1/3 C. leftover cooked chicken breasts, chopped
- 1 (16 oz.) packages coleslaw mix

Directions

1. Before you do anything preheat the oven to 350 F.
2. Crush the noodles and spread it on a lined up baking sheet.
3. Add to it the almonds with sunflower seeds and mix them. Cook them in the oven for 8 min while stirring them every 2 min.
4. Get a small mixing bowl: Whisk in it the seasoning packet, the oil, sugar, and vinegar to make the dressing.
5. Get a large mixing bowl: Combine in it the crunchy noodles mix with the chicken, coleslaw mix, and dressing. Toss them to coat.
6. Serve your salad right away.
7. Enjoy.

HOT APPLE
Ramen Salad

Prep Time: 5 mins
Total Time: 5 mins

Servings per Recipe: 12
Calories   217.6
Fat   14.1g
Cholesterol   0.0mg
Sodium   171.7mg
Carbohydrates   20.8g
Protein   3.0g

Ingredients
1/2 C. sugar
1/2 C. cooking oil
1/3 C. apple cider vinegar
2 ramen seasoning packets, from below packages
Garnish
1 lb coleslaw mix
2 (3 oz.) packages ramen noodles
1/4 C. slivered almonds, sautéed lightly
1/4 C. sunflower seeds
1/2 tsp onion powder

Directions
1. Get a small mixing bowl:
2. Whisk in it the sugar with oil, vinegar, and ramen seasoning packets.
3. Get a large mixing bowl: Combine in it the noodles after crushing it, the almonds, sunflower seeds, onion powder, and dressing. Toss them to coat.
4. Serve your salad right away.
5. Enjoy.

Hot Spinach Bowls

Prep Time: 5 mins
Total Time: 10 mins

Servings per Recipe: 4
Calories   208.0
Fat   7.0g
Cholesterol   0.0mg
Sodium   923.5mg
Carbohydrates   30.2g
Protein   7.2g

Ingredients

2 (3 oz.) packages ramen noodles, chicken
1 (10 oz.) packages frozen spinach,
chopped, thawed, drained

Directions

1. Prepare the noodles according to the directions on the package.
2. Stir in the spinach and cook it for an extra 2 min. Serve your soup hot.
3. Enjoy.

IRISH Ramen Pot Pie

🥣 Prep Time: 5 mins
🕒 Total Time: 25 mins

Servings per Recipe: 1
Calories   1030.4
Fat   56.6g
Cholesterol   154.2mg
Sodium   2069.6mg
Carbohydrates   72.7g
Protein   55.4g

Ingredients

1 (3-4 oz.) packages beef-flavored ramen noodles
2 tsp vegetable oil
1/2 lb ground beef
1/2 C. chopped onion
1/4 C. water
2 tsp Worcestershire sauce
1/2 C. frozen peas

Directions

1. Bring a large saucepan of water to a boil. Cook in it the noodles for 3 to 5 min or until it is done.
2. Place a large pan over medium heat. Heat the oil in it. Brown in it the beef for 6 min. Discard the excess fat.
3. Stir in the onion, water, Worcestershire sauce and peas, a pinch of salt and pepper. Mix them well. Cook them for 2 min.
4. Pour the mix in a greased baking dish. Lay the cooked noodles all over it. Cook it in the oven for 2 to 3 min. Serve your noodles casserole warm.
5. Enjoy.

Alternative Canadian Poutine

Prep Time: 5 mins
Total Time: 20 mins

Servings per Recipe: 1
Calories	682.5
Fat	37.7g
Cholesterol	48.3mg
Sodium	2740.1mg
Carbohydrates	60.7g
Protein	25.8g

Ingredients
- 1 (3-4 oz.) packages ramen noodles, any flavor
- 2 tsp vegetable oil
- 1/2-1 C. beef gravy
- 2-4 oz. shredded mozzarella cheese

Directions
1. Break the noodles into small pieces.
2. Place a large pan over medium heat. Heat the oil in it. Sauté in it the ramen for 2 to 3 min or until it becomes golden.
3. Drain it and place it in a greased casserole dish. Pour the gravy all over the noodles and sprinkle the cheese on top.
4. Cook the noodles casserole in the oven for 2 to 4 min or until the cheese melts. Serve it warm.
5. Enjoy.

EASY
Pad Thai Noodles

Prep Time: 5 mins
Total Time: 10 mins

Servings per Recipe: 1
Calories   603.5
Fat   27.2g
Cholesterol   241.7mg
Sodium   2533.5mg
Carbohydrates   65.1g
Protein   27.5g

Ingredients

1 (3-4 oz.) packages shrimp-flavored ramen noodles
6 medium shrimp
1 egg, lightly beaten
1 tsp fish sauce
1 lime, juice of
2 tbsp crushed peanuts
2 scallions, sliced thin
1/4 C. bean sprouts

Directions

1. Bring a large saucepan of water to a boil. Cook in it the noodles for 2 min. Stir in the shrimp and cook them for 3 to 4 min or until they are done.
2. Remove the pan from the heat and stir into it the egg while it is hot. Divide the soup between serving bowls.
3. Stir into them the lime juice with fish sauce. Garnish them with the peanuts, scallions and bean sprouts then serve them right away.
4. Enjoy.

Wavy Tuna Noodles

> Prep Time: 10 mins
> Total Time: 30 mins

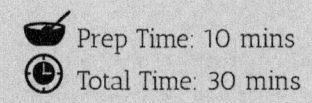

Servings per Recipe: 2
Calories	568.7
Fat	26.3g
Cholesterol	89.1mg
Sodium	1688.9mg
Carbohydrates	35.3g
Protein	46.0g

Ingredients
- 1 (3 oz.) packages chicken-flavored ramen noodles
- 1 (7 oz.) cans tuna
- 1 C. mixed vegetables, cooked
- 1 C. cheddar cheese, shredded
- 2 tbsp mayonnaise

Directions
1. Before you do anything preheat the oven to 350 F. Coat a baking dish with some butter or a cooking spray.
2. Prepare the noodles according to the directions on the package.
3. Get a large mixing bowl: Mix in it the tuna fish, the mixed vegetables, mayo, and the cheese. Drain the noodles and add it to the bowl then mix them well.
4. Pour the mix in the greased dish and cook them in the oven for 3 min. Serve your dish hot.
5. Enjoy.

CURRY
Coleslaw Ramen

Prep Time: 15 mins
Total Time: 30 mins

Servings per Recipe: 4
Calories 906.3
Fat 62.3g
Cholesterol 58.1mg
Sodium 1802.1mg
Carbohydrates 69.0g
Protein 21.1g

Ingredients

1/2 lb thinly sliced beef
1 tbsp olive oil
1 tsp toasted sesame oil
Vinaigrette
2-3 tbsp smooth cashew butter, or peanut butter
1/4 C. plain yogurt
2 tbsp mayonnaise
Salad
3-4 oz. chopped canned mild green chilies
15-16 oz. canned garbanzo beans, drained
2 garlic cloves, minced
2 tbsp dried onion flakes
1 tbsp soy sauce
2 tsp cider vinegar
1 tsp lemon juice, to taste
2 tsp mild curry powder, to taste
1/4 tsp cayenne, to taste
crushed red pepper flakes, to taste
1/8-1/4 tsp ground black pepper, to taste
1/4 C. slivered almonds
1/4 C. whole roasted cashews
3 green onions, chopped
1 tbsp toasted sesame seeds
1 (1 lb) bag coleslaw mix
2 (3 oz.) packages chicken-flavored ramen noodles
chopped roasted cashews, garnish

Directions

1. Place a large pan over medium heat. Heat in it the sesame and olive oil. Add the sliced beef and cook them for 3 to 6 min. Place it aside.
2. Get a large mixing bowl: Whisk in it the cashew butter with yogurt, and mayo to make the dressing.
3. Crush the noodles cook it according to the directions on the package for 2 min only.
4. Drain the noodles and add it to the bowl with the dressing along with the coleslaw veggies.
5. Toss them well to combine. Cover the bowl with a plastic wrap and place it in the fridge for 2 h.
6. Once the time is up, Adjust the seasoning of the salad. Serve it with your favorite toppings.
7. Enjoy.

Healing Black Ramen Broth

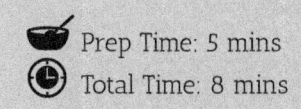

Prep Time: 5 mins
Total Time: 8 mins

Servings per Recipe: 2
Calories	8.8
Fat	0.0g
Cholesterol	0.0mg
Sodium	516.8mg
Carbohydrates	1.2g
Protein	1.0g

Ingredients
- 1 tsp bouillon
- 1 tbsp soy sauce
- 1/4 tsp garlic powder
- 1/2 tsp onion powder
- fresh ground black pepper, to taste
- miso, to taste
- 1 tsp black bean paste

Directions
1. Get a small mixing bowl: Combine in it the bouillon, soy sauce, garlic powder and onion powder.
2. Add the mix to the noodles while cooking it then serve it hot.
3. Enjoy.

HONEY
Ramen

Prep Time: 2 mins
Total Time: 17 mins

Servings per Recipe: 1
Calories 475.5
Fat 22.5g
Cholesterol 29.8mg
Sodium 1771.4mg
Carbohydrates 57.4g
Protein 11.3g

Ingredients
8 oz. water
1 (3 oz.) packets ramen noodles
1 tbsp butter
1/2 tbsp garlic powder
1/2 tbsp cayenne pepper
1/3 C. half-and-half cream
1-2 tbsps honey

Directions
1. Place a large pan over medium heat. Heat in it the sesame and olive oil. Add the sliced beef and cook them for 3 to 6 min. Place it aside.
2. Get a large mixing bowl: Whisk in it the cashew butter with yogurt, and mayo to make the dressing.
3. Crush the noodles cook it according to the directions on the package for 2 min only.
4. Drain the noodles and add it to the bowl with the dressing along with the coleslaw veggies.
5. Toss them well to combine. Cover the bowl with a plastic wrap and place it in the fridge for 2 h.
6. Once the time is up, Adjust the seasoning of the salad. Serve it with your favorite toppings.
7. Enjoy.

Chinese House Ramen

Prep Time: 5 mins
Total Time: 15 mins

Servings per Recipe: 1
Calories   11.0
Fat   0.2g
Cholesterol   0.0mg
Sodium   1.1mg
Carbohydrates   2.5g
Protein   0.4g

Ingredients
1/4 tsp season salt
1/4 tsp paprika
1/4 tsp smokehouse maple seasoning
1/4 tsp red cayenne pepper
full packet of ramen flavoring
1 dash black pepper
1 dried leaf basil
1 dash red cayenne pepper

ramen noodles

Directions
1. Bring a large saucepan of water to a boil. Stir in it 1/4 tsp of all seasonings and a seasoning packet.
2. Place the basil leaf in the hot broth then drain it and place it aside.
3. Place the noodles in the hot broth and let it cook for 1 to 2 min. Stir it and season it with a pinch of salt and pepper.
4. Pour the noodles into serving bowls. Garnish them with the basil leaves then serve them hot.
5. Enjoy.

RAMEN
Kyoto

Prep Time: 10 mins
Total Time: 20 mins

Servings per Recipe: 4
Calories   307.5
Fat   10.1g
Cholesterol   7.2mg
Sodium   2070.1mg
Carbohydrates   40.7g
Protein   13.0g

Ingredients

4 C. chicken stock
1 C. water
2 tbsp miso
6 oz. packaged ramen noodles
4 shiitake mushrooms, sliced thin
2 tbsp soy sauce
2 tbsp mirin
1/2 tsp garlic powder

1/4 tsp onion powder
1/4 C. scallion, green & white, sliced

Directions

1. Place a pot over medium heat. Stir in it the chicken stock, water, miso. Cook them until they start boiling.
2. Add the rest of the ingredients to the pot. Let them cook for 6 min. Stir in the scallions then serve your soup hot.
3. Enjoy.

Ramen Seafood Soup

🥣 Prep Time: 20 mins
🕐 Total Time: 45 mins

Servings per Recipe: 2
Calories   1120.1
Fat   31.5g
Cholesterol   137.1mg
Sodium   12292.4mg
Carbohydrates   118.7g
Protein   94.0g

Ingredients

- 1 tsp olive oil
- 1 tsp sesame oil
- 8 oz. brown button mushrooms
- 1 (3 oz.) packages ramen noodles
- 2 (8 oz.) halibut fillets
- kosher salt
- fresh ground pepper
- 1 tbsp honey
- 1 pinch chili flakes
- 6 medium shrimp, peeled and deveined
- 1/2 sweet onion, sliced
- 4 scallions, sliced
- 1 garlic clove, minced
- 2 tbsp soy sauce
- 1/4 C. mirin
- 2 C. miso

Directions

1. Before you do anything preheat the oven to 400 F.
2. Place a large skillet over medium heat. Heat the sesame and olive oil in it. Sauté in it the mushroom for 4 min. Drain it and place it aside.
3. Cut the ramen in half. Sprinkle halibut fillets with a pinch of salt and pepper. Coat them with the honey then sprinkle the chili flakes all over them.
4. Place a large piece of foil over each serving bowl to cover it completely. Place each half of the noodles in a serving bowl.
5. Top them with the halibut, shrimp, mushroom, and onion. Sprinkle the scallions on top.
6. Put the edges of the foil piece on top and seal them on top while making sure to leave a small opening on top of each pouch.
7. Get measuring C.: Mix in it the soy sauce, mirin and miso. Pour the mix in the opening of each pouch and pinch to close them.
8. Place the foil packets on a cookie pan and cook them in the oven for 24 min.
9. Once the time is up, place the packets back in the serving bowls. Serve them hot.
10. Enjoy.

FLORETS
Bunch Ramen

Prep Time: 5 mins
Total Time: 20 mins

Servings per Recipe: 2
Calories	176.4
Fat	8.8g
Cholesterol	24.1mg
Sodium	806.8mg
Carbohydrates	20.2g
Protein	5.9g

Ingredients
1 (10 oz.) cans cream of celery soup
1/2 C. milk
1 C. broccoli, pieces
1/2 C. cauliflower, pieces
1/2 C. sliced carrot
ramen noodles

Directions
1. Place a large saucepan over medium heat. Bring it the milk to a boil. Add the veggies to it then lower the heat and let them cook for 16 min.
2. Prepare the noodles according to the directions on the package. Drain it and divide it between the serving bowls.
3. Once the time is up, stir the celery soup into the saucepan. Cook them for 2 min.
4. Pour the creamy veggies soup over the noodles. Serve it hot.
5. Enjoy.

Japanese Restaurant Ramen

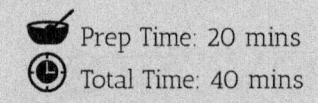

🥣 Prep Time: 20 mins
⏲ Total Time: 40 mins

Servings per Recipe: 4
Calories   825.0
Fat   36.3g
Cholesterol   293.2mg
Sodium   8532.8mg
Carbohydrates   65.2g
Protein   62.1g

Ingredients

Miso
200 g white miso
200 g brown miso
Egg
100 ml regular soy sauce
100 ml water
10 g sugar
4 soft-boiled eggs, peeled
Bamboo
200 g bamboo shoots, drained
5 g sesame oil
100 g regular soy sauce

Base
10 g sugar
2 g red chili pepper flakes
1 1/4 liters hot chicken stock, strained
400 g cooked chicken
110 g ramen noodles
200 g bean sprouts, blanched
100 g frozen corn kernels, thawed drained
10 g wakame seaweed, soaked for 1 h
60 g unsalted butter, cut into four equal slices
20 g chives, thinly sliced

Directions

1. Get a small mixing bowl: Whisk in it the white and brown miso. Place it aside.
2. Get a large mixing bowl: Whisk in it the soy, water and sugar to make the marinade. Place in it the peeled eggs and let them sit for 4 h to an overnight.
3. Place a small pan over medium heat. Heat the sesame oil in it. Add the bamboo and cook it for 2 min. Stir in the rest of the veggies and pulled chicken. Cook them for 4 min.
4. Prepare the noodles according to the directions on the package.
5. Pour the miso in serving bowls. Add to them the hot stock and mix them well.
6. Drain the noodles and add it to the stock right away. Top them with the veggies stir fry. Serve your ramen noodles hot.
7. Enjoy.

AKARI'S Favorite

Prep Time: 1 mins
Total Time: 8 mins

Servings per Recipe: 1
Calories   1118.1
Fat   55.7g
Cholesterol   107.6mg
Sodium   3759.4mg
Carbohydrates   113.4g
Protein   39.9g

Ingredients
2 (3 oz.) packages oriental-flavor instant ramen noodles, with flavor packs
5 C. hot tap water
1/8 C. coarse chopped yellow onion
sriracha sauce
1 tbsp butter
1/2 tsp garlic powder
1/4 lb ground beef

Directions
1. Place a large saucepan over medium heat. Heat in it the water until it starts boiling. Cut the noodles in half and place it in the hot water.
2. Let it cook for 4 min without stirring it.
3. Place a small skillet over medium heat. Melt 1 tbsp of butter in it. Add the beef with garlic powder and cook them for 4 to 5 min. Discard the excess fat.
4. Stir the onion into the noodles. Drain them and transfer them with 2 C. of cooking liquid into a serving bowl.
5. Add to them the seasoning packets and stir them well. Top the hot soup with the cooked beef mix. Serve them hot.
6. Enjoy.

Ramen for 2

Prep Time: 10 mins
Total Time: 25 mins

Servings per Recipe: 2
Calories   274.0
Fat   8.5g
Cholesterol   26.2mg
Sodium   928.7mg
Carbohydrates   34.3g
Protein   16.0g

Ingredients

2 1/2 oz. ramen noodles, no packet
1/2 C. low sodium chicken broth
1 1/2 tsp low sodium soy sauce
1/3 C. frozen peas
1/3 C. drained canned corn
1/2 C. shredded cooked chicken
1/2 tsp cornstarch
1 scallion, thinly sliced

Directions

1. Prepare the noodles according to the directions on the package.
2. Place a large saucepan over medium heat. Stir in it the broth, soy sauce, peas, corn and chicken. Simmer them for 3 min.
3. Get a small mixing bowl: Mix in it the cornstarch with 1 tsp cold water. Stir it into the pan. Cook the soup for 1 min while stirring all the time.
4. Drain the noodles and stir it into the soup with the scallions. Cook them for 1 min then serve it hot.
5. Enjoy.

MILANESE Casserole

Prep Time: 5 mins
Total Time: 35 mins

Servings per Recipe: 4
Calories 531.9
Fat 29.5g
Cholesterol 108.4mg
Sodium 1302.4mg
Carbohydrates 28.3g
Protein 36.1g

Ingredients

2 (3 oz.) packages beef-flavor ramen noodles
1 lb lean ground beef
24 slices pepperoni
1 (14 1/2 oz.) cans diced tomatoes with basil, garlic and oregano, undrained
1 C. water
1 small green bell pepper, cut into 1/2-inch pieces
1 C. shredded mozzarella cheese

Directions

1. Place a large pan over medium heat. Brown in it the beef with pepperoni for 9 to 11 min while stirring them from time to time.
2. Discard the excess fat. Add the water, tomato, and seasoning packet. Bring them to a boil. Add the noodles with bell pepper. Let them cook for 4 to 6 min.
3. Top the noodles skillet with the cheese then put on the lid. Let it cook for 6 min. Serve it hot.
4. Enjoy.

Monterey Ramen

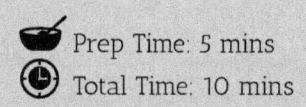

Prep Time: 5 mins
Total Time: 10 mins

Servings per Recipe: 2
Calories	312.1
Fat	13.3g
Cholesterol	29.5mg
Sodium	741.4mg
Carbohydrates	27.9g
Protein	19.4g

Ingredients
- 1 (3 oz.) packages chicken-flavored ramen noodles
- 1 1/2 C. water
- 1 (3 oz.) cans light chunk tuna in water
- 1/3-1/2 C. Monterey jack cheese, shredded
- 1/8-1/4 tsp garlic powder

Directions
1. Get a 2 quarts microwave proof bowl: Stir in it the water with noodles, and seasoning packet. Cook them in the microwave for 6 min.
2. Once the time is up, stir into it the cheese with tuna while it is hot. Season it with the garlic powder then serve it hot.
3. Enjoy.

RAMEN
Sake

Prep Time: 1 mins
Total Time: 11 mins

Servings per Recipe: 1
Calories 432.7
Fat 14.5g
Cholesterol 0.0mg
Sodium 1893.8mg
Carbohydrates 58.3g
Protein 9.0g

Ingredients
1 C. water
1 tbsp Shoyu (soy sauce)
1 fluid oz. sake
1 (3 oz.) package ramen noodles

Directions
1. Place a large saucepan over medium heat. Stir in it the water, shoyu, and sake. Cook them until they start boiling.
2. Stir in it the noodles without the seasoning packet. Let it cook for 5 min. Once the time is up, serve it hot.
3. Enjoy.

Japanese Ramen Burgers

Prep Time: 20 mins
Total Time: 60 mins

Servings per Recipe: 3
Calories   742
Fat   55.7g
Cholesterol   417mg
Sodium   1816mg
Carbohydrates   13.4g
Protein   45.9

Ingredients

2 (3 oz.) packages instant ramen noodles, flavor packet discarded
2 large eggs
salt and ground black pepper to taste
3/4 lb lean ground beef
1 tbsp soy sauce
1 tsp sesame oil
3 tbsp vegetable oil, divided
3 slices American cheese
1/4 C. ketchup
2 tbsp chile-garlic sauce
1 1/2 C. arugula
3 large eggs

Directions

1. Bring a large pot of water to a boil. Cook in it the ramen noodles for 4 min. Remove the noodles from the water and place it aside.
2. Get a large mixing bowl: Whisk in it the eggs with a pinch of salt and pepper. Stir in it the cooked noodles.
3. Pour the noodles mix into 6 greased ramekins. Cover the pan completely with a plastic wrap and place it in the fridge for 22 min.
4. Get a mixing bowl: Combine in it the beef, soy sauce, and sesame oil. Shape the mix into 3 burgers.
5. Place a large pan over medium heat. Heat in it 1 tbsp of oil in it. Cook in it the noodles buns for 3 to 4 min on each side.
6. Drain them and place them aside. Heat 1 tbsp of oil in the same pan. Cook in it the beef burgers for 4 to 5 min on each side.
7. Get a small mixing bowls: Whisk in it the ketchup and chile-garlic sauce.
8. Lather the sauce mix over the noodles patties. Lay the arugula leaves on burger buns then top it with the noodles buns and beef patties.
9. Heat 1 tsp of oil in a small pan. Fry in it the eggs for 2 to 3 min on each side. Place them over the beef patties and cover them with the upper buns.
10. Serve your burgers right away.
11. Enjoy.

RAMEN SUMMER
Salad with Soy Sauce Vinaigrette

Prep Time: 10 mins
Total Time: 12 mins

Servings per Recipe: 6
Calories 618
Fat 44g
Cholesterol 20mg
Sodium 1102mg
Carbohydrates 50.3g
Protein 10.3g

Ingredients
Salad Dressing:
1/2 C. canola oil
1/2 C. white sugar
1/4 C. red wine vinegar
2 tbsp soy sauce
Salad:
1/4 C. butter
2 tbsp white sugar

2 (3 oz.) packages ramen noodles
1/2 C. sesame seeds
3 oz. slivered almonds
1 tbsp soy sauce
2 large heads bok choy, chopped
6 green onions, chopped

Directions
1. Get a mixing bowl: Whisk in it the canola oil, sugar, red wine vinegar, and 2 tbsp soy sauce to make the dressing.
2. Place a medium pot over medium heat. Heat the butter in it until it melts. Add to it the sugar and stir until it melts.
3. Crush the noodles and add it to the pot. Mix in the seasoning packet, sesame seeds, almonds, and soy sauce. Cook them for 3 min while stirring all the time.
4. Remove the pot from the heat. Stir in the dressing with bok choy, and green onions. Serve your warm salad right away.
5. Enjoy.

Enoki Soup

Prep Time: 20 mins
Total Time: 44 mins

Servings per Recipe: 1
Calories 495
Fat 7.8g
Cholesterol 10mg
Sodium 4865mg
Carbohydrates 85g
Protein 23.4g

Ingredients

- 5 green beans
- 1 tsp olive oil
- 1 tbsp chopped garlic
- 2 C. chicken broth
- 2 C. water
- 1 red finger chile pepper, sliced
- 2 cloves garlic, sliced
- 1 tbsp soy sauce
- 1 tbsp fish sauce
- 1 tbsp ground black pepper
- 1 tsp rice wine vinegar
- 1 (3 oz.) package ramen noodles (Korean Style preferred)
- 1 (3 oz.) package enoki mushrooms, halved
- 3 scallions, chopped
- 1/3 C. whole Thai basil leaves
- 1/4 C. whole cilantro leaves

Directions

1. Place a large saucepan of water over medium heat. Heat it until it starts boiling.
2. Cook in it the green beans for 3 min. Remove the beans from the water and place it aside.
3. Place a large saucepan over medium heat. Heat the olive oil in it. Add the garlic and cook it for 1 min.
4. Stir in the broth, water, red chile pepper. Cook them until they start boiling. Let them cook for 4 min.
5. Add the soy sauce, fish sauce, black pepper, and rice wine vinegar to the pot. Let them cook for an extra 3 min.
6. Fold the green beans, ramen noodles, and seasoning packet into the saucepan. Cook them for 2 min.
7. Add the scallions with mushroom into the soup and cook them for 3 min.
8. Serve your soup hot.
9. Enjoy.

JAPANESE
Risotto

🍳 Prep Time: 5 mins
🕐 Total Time: 20 mins

Servings per Recipe: 4
Calories 297
Fat 20.4g
Cholesterol 35mg
Sodium 746mg
Carbohydrates 15.4g
Protein 13.2g

Ingredients

1/2 C. diced turkey bacon
1 tbsp olive oil
1 medium onion, chopped
1/4 tsp salt
1 (3 oz.) package ramen noodles, coarsely broken in package, packet removed
1 (10 oz.) package frozen peas
3 C. low-sodium chicken broth

1 tbsp butter
1/2 C. grated Parmesan cheese, plus additional for serving
1/4 tsp ground black pepper

Directions

1. Place a large pan over medium heat. Cook in it the bacon for 6 min while stirring all the time.
2. Stir in the onion and cook it for 3 min. Combine in the ramen and cook it for 2 min.
3. Stir in the broth with peas and cook them until they start boiling. Cook them for 4 min while stirring them from time to time.
4. Turn off the heat and add the butter, Parmesan, and pepper. Serve your risotto skillet hot.
5. Enjoy.

Hot Ramen Spread

🥣 Prep Time: 10 mins
🕐 Total Time: 1 hr 15 mins

Servings per Recipe: 10
Calories   237
Fat   21.1g
Cholesterol   29mg
Sodium   578mg
Carbohydrates   3.9g
Protein   8.2g

Ingredients
3 (3 oz.) packages beef-flavored ramen noodles
boiling water to cover
1 C. mayonnaise
1 (4 oz.) can diced jalapeno peppers
1 (12 oz.) can chicken breast, drained and shredded
1/2 (7 oz.) bottle hot sauce

Directions
1. Get a large mixing bowl: Crush the noodles and toss it with the seasoning packets in it.
2. Cover the noodles with some hot water and let it sit for 6 min.
3. Get a small mixing bowl: Whisk in it the mayonnaise, chicken, jalapeno peppers, and hot sauce.
4. Drain the noodles and add it to the sauce mix. Stir them well. Place the spread in the fridge for 1 h then serve it.
5. Enjoy.

SKINNY GIRL
Cabbage Salad

Prep Time: 15 mins
Total Time: 15 mins

Servings per Recipe: 10
Calories 227
Fat 18.2g
Cholesterol 0mg
Sodium 169mg
Carbohydrates 14.3g
Protein 3.4g

Ingredients
1 (3 oz.) package ramen noodle, crushed
8 oz. cabbage, shredded
4 oz. slivered almonds
1/4 C. sunflower seeds
2 green onions, sliced
1/2 C. vegetable oil
1/3 C. cider vinegar
1/4 C. white sugar

Directions
1. Get a small mixing bowl: Whisk in it the oil, vinegar and sugar.
2. Get a large mixing bowl: Toss in it the cabbage, almonds, sunflower seeds and green onion. Add the dressing and toss them to coat.
3. Serve your salad right away.
4. Enjoy.

Sesame Land

Prep Time: 10 mins
Total Time: 20 mins

Servings per Recipe: 8
Calories	364
Fat	27g
Cholesterol	8mg
Sodium	911mg
Carbohydrates	28.3g
Protein	5.8g

Ingredients

- 2 tbsp butter
- 3/4 C. blanched slivered almonds
- 1/2 C. sesame seeds
- 1 medium head cabbage, chopped
- 8 green onion, chopped
- 2 (3 oz.) packages ramen noodles
- 1/2 C. vegetable oil
- 1/2 C. white sugar
- 1/3 C. rice wine vinegar
- 1/4 tsp ground black pepper
- 2 tsp salt

Directions

1. Place a large pan over low heat. Heat the butter in it until it melts. Toast in it the sesame seeds and almonds for 2 to 4 min.
2. Get a small mixing bowl: Mix in it the oil, sugar, vinegar, pepper and salt to make the dressing.
3. Get a large mixing bowl: Toss in it the cabbage, onions, almonds, sesame seeds and crushed ramen noodles.
4. Add the dressing and toss them to coat. Serve your salad right away.
5. Enjoy.

BALSAMIC Golden Noodles

Prep Time: 20 mins
Total Time: 50 mins

Servings per Recipe: 6
Calories 527
Fat 33g
Cholesterol 0mg
Sodium 491mg
Carbohydrates 51.3g
Protein 10.3g

Ingredients

1/2 C. canola oil
1/2 C. white sugar
1/4 C. water
1/4 C. balsamic vinegar
2 (3 oz.) packages chicken-flavored ramen noodles, crushed, seasoning packets reserved
1 (12 oz.) package broccoli coleslaw mix
1 bunch green onions, sliced
1 C. roasted cashews
1/4 C. roasted sunflower seed kernels

Directions

1. Get a small mixing bowl: Combine in it the canola oil, sugar, water, balsamic vinegar, and seasoning packets.
2. Get a large mixing bowl: Combine in it the noodles with broccoli slaw and green onions. Add the dressing and toss to coat. Let the salad sit for 30 min or more.
3. Sprinkle over it the cashews and sunflower seeds. Serve it right away.
4. Enjoy.

Sendai Salad

Prep Time: 10 mins
Total Time: 10 mins

Servings per Recipe: 6
Calories 429
Fat 28g
Cholesterol 0mg
Sodium 337mg
Carbohydrates 38g
Protein 10.9g

Ingredients

1 medium head cabbage, shredded
1 bunch green onions, chopped
2 (3 oz.) packages chicken flavored ramen noodles
4 oz. slivered almonds, toasted
1/2 C. olive oil
2 tbsp white sugar
3 tbsp distilled white vinegar

Directions

1. Get a small mixing bowl: Mix in it the oil, sugar, vinegar and seasoning packets.
2. Get a large mixing bowl: Toss in it the cabbage, green onions, noodles and almonds. Add the dressing and mix them well. Serve your salad right away.
3. Enjoy.

CHICKEN BREASTS
Soup on a Ramen Beach

Prep Time: 20 mins
Total Time: 45 mins

Servings per Recipe: 8
Calories 551
Fat 24.2g
Cholesterol 45mg
Sodium 1646mg
Carbohydrates 56.5g
Protein 29.8g

Ingredients

1 fresh lemongrass stalk, outer leaves removed
2 quarts chicken stock
1/2 C. minced fresh ginger, divided
4 fresh kaffir lime leaves
1 tbsp minced garlic
1 tbsp Sriracha chile sauce
1 1/2 lb skinless, boneless chicken breast halves, cut into 1-inch strips
1/2 C. fresh cilantro, bundled
2 (14 oz.) cans coconut milk
3 tbsp brown sugar
2 tbsp lime juice
1 tbsp fish sauce
6 (3 oz.) packages ramen noodles, packets removed
2 large carrots, shredded
1 C. chopped tomatoes
3 green onions, chopped
1/4 C. chopped fresh cilantro, or to taste

Directions

1. Crunch the lower 2/3 of a lemongrass stalk with the back of a spoon then mince the rest of it slightly.
2. Place a large saucepan over medium heat. Stir in the stock with minced lemongrass, bruised lemongrass stalk, 1/2 the ginger, lime leaves, garlic, and Sriracha sauce.
3. Cook them until they start boiling. Lower the heat and bring them to a simmer. Add the chicken breasts and cook them for 12 min.
4. Discard the lemongrass stalk and lime leaves. Stir the cilantro into the broth and cook it for 3 min.
5. Stir in the coconut milk, remaining ginger, brown sugar, lime juice, and fish sauce. Drain the cilantro and discard it. Let the chicken soup cook for 8 min.
6. Cook the ramen according to the directions on the package without the seasoning packets.
7. Drain the noodles and divide it between serving bowls. Stir the carrots, tomatoes, and green onions into soup. Pour it all over the noodles.
8. Serve your soup bowls hot.
9. Enjoy.

Kimchi and Sausage Ramen

Prep Time: 30 mins
Total Time: 57 mins

Servings per Recipe: 6
Calories 697
Fat 45.7g
Cholesterol 97mg
Sodium 4194mg
Carbohydrates 40.9g
Protein 30.9g

Ingredients
1 (12 oz.) can turkey spam lunch meat
14 oz. smoked beef sausage, sliced
1 large onion, sliced
6 oz. kimchi
1/4 C. Korean red pepper powder
3 tbsp soy sauce
3 tbsp gochujang
5 cloves garlic, minced
1 pinch ground black pepper
1 bunch green onions, chopped
2 (32 oz.) containers chicken broth
7 3/4 oz. ramen noodles
1 slice American cheese

Directions
1. Place the luncheon meat on 2 sides of the pot leaving the middle of it empty. Top it with the sausage, onion, and kimchee.
2. Get a small mixing bowl: Whisk in it the red pepper powder, soy sauce, gochujang, garlic, and black pepper. Fill the empty space in the pot with the mix.
3. Top everything with the green onion. Stir in the chicken broth and cook them until they start boiling.
4. Cook the ramen according to the directions on the package without the seasoning packets.
5. Drain the noodles and add it to the pot. Let them cook for 6 min. serve your soup with some shredded American cheese.
6. Enjoy.

SYRIAN INSPIRED
Ramen with Grape Leaves

Prep Time: 5 mins
Total Time: 15 mins

Servings per Recipe: 1
Calories   460
Fat   21.3g
Cholesterol   26mg
Sodium   4605mg
Carbohydrates   50.3g
Protein   10.3g

Ingredients

1/2 C. orange juice
1 (3 oz.) package chicken-flavored ramen noodles
3 large grape leaves
1/4 onion, cut into large chunks
3 tbsp soy sauce
3 tbsp coconut-flavored rum, optional
2 tbsp Syrian za'atar spice
1 tbsp sesame oil
1 1/2 tsp red pepper flakes

1 tsp barbeque sauce, or to taste
2 garlic cloves, minced
1 bouillon cube
water, to cover

Directions

1. Place a pot over medium heat:
2. Combine in it the orange juice, ramen noodles and seasoning packet, grape leaves, onion, soy sauce, rum, za'atar, sesame oil, red pepper flakes, barbeque sauce, garlic cloves, and bouillon cube.
3. Cook them until they start boiling. Lower the heat and put on the lid. Cook the soup for 12 min. Serve it hot.
4. Enjoy.

July's Chicken Salad

Prep Time: 25 mins
Total Time: 25 mins

Servings per Recipe: 10
Calories 342
Fat 27.1g
Cholesterol 22mg
Sodium 409mg
Carbohydrates 15.5g
Protein 11.2g

Ingredients

1 head cabbage, shredded
2 cooked skinless, boneless chicken breast halves, cubed
6 tbsp balsamic vinegar
2 chicken-flavored ramen noodle seasoning packets
1/4 C. white sugar
1 C. olive oil
6 green onions, chopped
1/4 C. toasted sliced almonds, or to taste
1/4 C. toasted sesame seeds, or to taste

Directions

1. Get a large mixing bowl: Toss in it the chicken and cabbage.
2. Get a small mixing bowl: Mix in it the vinegar, ramen noodle seasoning, and sugar to make the dressing. Add the olive oil while mixing all the time.
3. Fold the green onions into the dressing.
4. Crush the noodles and cook it according to the directions on the package. Drain it and add it to the salad with the dressing.
5. Toss the salad to coat. Fold the almonds and sesame seeds into the salad. Serve it right away.
6. Enjoy.

SOUTHWEST
Ramen Casserole

Prep Time: 20 mins
Total Time: 50 mins

Servings per Recipe: 8
Calories	811
Fat	46.9g
Cholesterol	119mg
Sodium	1298mg
Carbohydrates	60.1g
Protein	39g

Ingredients

1 lb skinless, boneless chicken breast halves
3 (3 oz.) packages chicken flavored ramen noodles
1 (13 oz.) package Ranch-flavored tortilla chips
1 (10.75 oz.) can condensed cream of mushroom soup
2 C. sour cream
1 C. milk
1 (16 oz.) package frozen broccoli florets, thawed
4 C. shredded Cheddar cheese

Directions

1. Before you do anything preheat the oven to 325 F.
2. Place a large pot over medium heat. Stir in the chicken with the ramen seasoning packets. Cover them with water and cook them until they start boiling.
3. Let them cook for 10 to 14 min or until the chicken is done. Drain the chicken and cut it into dices.
4. Stir the ramen noodles into the same pot. Let it cook for 3 min.
5. Get a mixing bowl: Whisk in it the cream of mushroom soup, sour cream and milk to make the sauce.
6. Coat a casserole dish with some butter.
7. Lay 1/3 of the tortilla chips in the bottom of the casserole followed by 1/2 of the noodles, 1/2 of the chicken, 1/2 of the broccoli, 1/3 of the cheese, and 1/2 of the soup mixture.
8. Repeat the process with the remaining ingredients to make another layer.
9. Place the casserole in the oven and let it cook for 32 min. serve it hot.
10. Enjoy.

Ramen On Fire

Prep Time: 10 mins
Total Time: 22 mins

Servings per Recipe: 1
Calories   315
Fat   1.9g
Cholesterol   0mg
Sodium   939mg
Carbohydrates   60.7g
Protein   14.6g

Ingredients
- 2 C. water
- 1/2 jalapeno pepper, very thinly sliced
- 1 (3 oz.) package chicken-flavored ramen noodles
- 2 mushrooms, thinly sliced
- 3 wedges lime, juiced
- 1 green onion, sliced
- 1 tbsp cilantro leaves
- 1/4 tsp garlic chile paste
- 1/8 tsp sesame oil

Directions
1. Place a large saucepan over medium heat. Heat in it the water until it id boiling. Add the jalapeno and cook it for 3 min.
2. Stir in the noodles with the seasoning packet and mushroom. Let them cook for 6 min.
3. Spoon the mix into serving bowls. Top your ramen bowls with lime juice, green onion, cilantro, garlic chile paste, and sesame oil. Serve them hot.
4. Enjoy.

RAMEN
Salad Bowl

Prep Time: 20 mins
Total Time: 20 mins

Servings per Recipe: 6
Calories 55
Fat 0.8g
Cholesterol < 1mg
Sodium 21mg
Carbohydrates 10.2g
Protein 2.1g

Ingredients
2 C. shredded red cabbage
1/2 red onion, thinly sliced
2 red bell peppers, diced
1 C. sliced sugar snap peas
2 green onions, thinly sliced
1 red jalapeno pepper, finely minced
5 radishes, diced
5 strawberries, diced
1 tbsp crushed ramen noodles
1 tbsp slivered almonds

Directions
1. Get a large mixing bowl: Toss in it the red cabbage, red onions, red peppers, sugar snap peas, green onions, jalapeno peppers, and radishes.
2. Top the salad with the strawberries, ramen noodles, and almonds. Serve your salad right away.
3. Enjoy.

Ramen in College II

Prep Time: 2 mins
Total Time: 7 mins

Servings per Recipe: 2
Calories	334
Fat	15.5g
Cholesterol	39mg
Sodium	1266mg
Total Carbohydrates	27.8g
Protein	20.3g

Ingredients
- 1 C. boiling water
- 1 (3 oz.) package any flavor ramen noodles
- 1 (3 oz.) can water-packed tuna, drained
- 2 slices American cheese

Directions
1. Get a microwave safe bowl: fill it with 1 C. of boiling water. Stir in it the noodles and cook it for 2 to 3 min in the microwave.
2. Pour the noodles in a colander to drain it.
3. Get a large mixing bowl: Stir in it the noodles with then seasoning packet, tuna, and American cheese.
4. Cook the noodles for an extra 2 min in the microwave. Serve it hot.
5. Enjoy.

ENJOY THE RECIPES?

KEEP ON COOKING
WITH 6 MORE FREE COOKBOOKS!

Visit our website and simply enter your email address to join the club and receive your 6 cookbooks.

http://booksumo.com/magnet

Printed in Great Britain
by Amazon